WICCAN MAGICK

The Inner Teachings Revealed

Raven Grimassi reveals initiate-level teachings gathered over the course of twenty-five years of study and practice—and gives seekers a rare opportunity to access Wicca's most ancient inner teachings. Wiccan Magick is a complete study of all aspects of magickal practice and belief:

- Uncover the mystical meanings of Wiccan concepts and objects

- Understand the secret inner mechanisms of Wiccan magick

- Explore the "why" of Wiccan concepts

- Enhance your own magical workings by fully understanding how the spells and rituals work

- Learn the inherent occult properties of natural objects—and how to tap their power

- Explore folk magick, herbal magick, mineral magick, the elements, the astral realm, the odic force, and lunar and solar consciousness

About the Author

Trained in the Family Tradition of Italian Witchcraft as well as Gardnerian Wicca, Brittic Wicca, and the Pictish-Gaelic Tradition, Raven Grimassi has been a teacher and practitioner for over twenty-five years. He is currently Directing Elder of the Arician Ways. It is his life's work to ensure survival of traditional material. He was the editor of *Raven's Call* magazine (1992–1995), a journal of pre-Christian European Religion, and has been a writer and editor for several other magazines. He lectures and teaches workshops and classes on the practices and natures of Wicca and Witchcraft, and has appeared on television and radio talk shows in the San Diego area.

To Write to the Author

If you wish to contact the author or would like more information about this book, please write to the author in care of Llewellyn Worldwide, and we will forward your request. Both the author and publisher appreciate hearing from you and learning of your enjoyment of this book and how it has helped you. Llewellyn Worldwide cannot guarantee that every letter written to the author can be answered, but all will be forwarded. Please write to:

Raven Grimassi
c/o Llewellyn Worldwide Ltd.
P.O. Box 64383, Dept. K255–0
St. Paul, MN 55164–0383, U.S.A.

Please enclose a self-addressed, stamped envelope for reply or $1.00 to cover costs. If outside the U.S.A., enclose international postal reply coupon.

RAVEN GRIMASSI

WICCAN MAGICK

Inner Teachings of the Craft

2004
Llewellyn Publications
St. Paul, Minnesota 55164–0383, U.S.A.

FIRST EDITION
Sixth Printing, 2004

Cover design by Tom Grewe
Cover art by Paul Mason
Illustrations by Shadowhawk
Interior design and editing by Connie Hill

Library of Congress Cataloging-in-Publication Data
Grimassi, Raven. 1951–
    Wiccan magick : inner teachings of the craft / Raven
Grimassi. — 1st ed.
        p.   cm. —
    Includes bibliographical references and index.
    ISBN 1–56718–255–0 (trade pbk.)
    1. Witchcraft.   2. Magick.   I. Title.
BF1566.G74   1998
133.4′3—dc21   98–37833
                                                              CIP

Llewellyn Worldwide does not participate in, endorse, or have any authority or responsibility concerning private business transactions between our authors and the public.
    All mail addressed to the author is forwarded but the publisher cannot, unless specifically instructed by the author, give out an address or phone number.

Llewellyn Publications
A Division of Llewellyn Worldwide, Ltd.
St. Paul, Minnesota, 55164–0383, U.S.A.
www.llewellyn.com

Printed in the United States of America

Dedication

To the members of Clan Umbrea,
who through the walk of Light and Darkness
have remained my true companions on the Path.

———————

Other Books by the Author

The Book of the Holy Strega (Nemi Enterprises, 1981)

The Book of Ways, Vols. I & II (Nemi Enterprises, 1982)

Whispers, the Teachers of Old Italy
  (Moon Dragon Publishing, 1991)

Teachings of the Holy Strega (Moon Dragon Publishing, 1991)

Wiccan Mysteries (Llewellyn Publications, 1997)

Hereditary Witchcraft (Llewellyn Publications, 1999)

Italian Witchcraft (previously titled *Ways of the Strega)*
  (Llewellyn Publications,1995, 2000)

Encyclopedia of Wicca & Witchcraft (Llewellyn Publications, 2000)

The Witches' Craft (Llewellyn Publications, 2002)

The Witch's Familiar (Llewellyn Publications, 2003)

Spirit of the Witch (Llewellyn Publications, 2003)

Acknowledgments

I wish to thank my long-time friend Donald Michael Kraig, author of *Modern Magick,* for reading my manuscript and for his helpful suggestions on how to improve the material. I also want to thank the many teachers I've had the honor to study with, some of whom were students who taught me more than I ever taught them. Finally, I wish to thank my ever vigilant critics who inspire me to strive toward becoming a better writer and researcher.

Contents

Introduction

My purpose in this book is to provide the reader with an understanding of the inner mechanisms of Wiccan magick. The following chapters present a blend of magickal concepts constituting an inner magickal tradition within Wicca. Modern Wicca is an extremely eclectic religion; today we find many elements comprising what was once a simplistic, ancient Pagan fertility cult. Because modern Wicca embraces many traditions, from many different cultures, it is difficult to do justice to each one in the scope of a single volume such as this book. What I offer here is an overview of basic initiate-level concepts as I have found them within several Wiccan traditions.

I believe that it is just as important to understand why something works as it is to understand how something works. Many books will provide you with instructions on how to cast a spell or perform a ritual, but few provide an understanding of why the spells or rituals work. I believe that such an understanding greatly empowers a person's ability to create or enhance his or her own magickal workings.

In this book you will discover the inherent occult properties of natural objects and the means by which their power can be tapped. The secrets of lunar light and lunar magnetism are revealed in this book, along with techniques to bind or release this ancient energy source. You will also discover why bonfires and candles came to be used in Wiccan magick and how they affect spells and rituals.

The powers of the mind are essential to the practice of magick. A magickal mentality serves to connect the practitioner to higher sources of power. Therefore I have included in this book several chapters dealing with lunar and solar consciousness, as well as magickal reasoning and lifestyle. To live and walk a magickal path is to see the world around you in a different light.

I think it is important to understand the evolution of the Craft and to comprehend the various aspects included in ritual, spell casting, and general theology. When we understand why something exists within a ritual structure, we can better understand how to build on the underlying concepts. These concepts reflect the wisdom of those who came before us; we can join in partnership with our ancestors and aid the continuance of Wiccan practices as we adapt them to new environments. When an organism stops growing it begins to die. It is essential for new growth that the roots be sound and healthy. Therefore, it is wise to blend the old ways with the new ways, abandoning neither.

In modern Wicca we find two main branches of practice: Ceremonial and Shamanic. Ceremonial magick is largely built on techniques, concepts, and rituals established by ancient practitioners. Shamanic Wicca is built mainly on intuitive, self-directed methods, although still incorporating ancient techniques such as drumming, fasting, and trance inducement. Ceremonial magick has evolved from Shamanic practices that were refined over countless centuries of magickal practice.

The concepts in this book are drawn from those teachings and practices that survived the test of time. The modern practitioner need not be bound to this structure, but will find value in the teachings reflected here. For the Shamanic Wiccan, this book provides a study of the areas that the ancient practitioners felt were important to focus on. The elements described here can serve as a guide, directing the practitioner toward mapping out the modern relevance of surviving concepts and structures. What was important to our ancestors is still important to their descendants.

Ceremonial Wiccans will find more than familiar structure and theology in this book. They will rediscover the spiritual and magickal forces that empower all that has been passed down to us. It is easy to perform the rites as we have in the past and to grow dispassionate toward them, but it is the inner mechanisms within them that give life and animate the current flowing through the rituals. This is an ancient current flowing from the past to the present. My purpose in writing this book is to encourage us all to look again beneath the waters and to rediscover the teeming life within.

To walk the path of Wiccan magick is to align oneself with the ways of Nature. Through alignment we come to understand the ways of Mother Earth. In this mentality we find that Nature is the reflective blueprint of divine creation. Understanding this, we can then discern the patterns within Nature and realize that her ways and laws are themselves reflections of a higher principle. In this we find that all things are connected. In connectivity we are never alone, for we belong to the community of souls. Spirits and guides walk with us, and our journey is directed from within and from without. Let us therefore turn now to the well-worn path. From there we shall blaze new trails and walk the path of Wiccan magick together.

Chapter One

The Old Ways

The Old Ways speak of connectivity to the Source-of-All-Things. They teach that Divinity is reflected in Nature, and Nature is reflected in the diversity of life-forms within it. The Old Ways reveal that Nature is the Great Teacher.

When Gerald Gardner's writings first came to public attention in 1954, he called Wicca *The Old Religion*. The Old Religion evolved out of primitive Neolithic beliefs and concepts, eventually evolving into a European Mystery Tradition containing the accumulated knowledge and wisdom of many generations. The ancient pre-Christian European Mysteries are the very roots of modern Wicca. These Mysteries form the foundation of modern Wiccan ritual and magickal practices, and it is from these ancient roots that we draw the nourishment that allows for new growth.

Magick and religion arose out of humankind's attempts to understand the world in which they existed. To our ancestors, the ever-returning cycles of Nature and the unnamed laws of cause and effect all seemed to suggest an established order to the Universe. Certain foods satisfied and others did not. Some techniques brought about a successful hunt and other techniques failed to do so. The ancients thought that surely something must be in control of these things. If this were true, then perhaps there were ways to encourage this mysterious aid.

A structured belief system incorporating various gods and spirits evolved from primitive beliefs in unseen forces. Natural objects became associated with desired effects, and over the course of time a list of magickal charms resulted. With these items, specifically favored by a certain deity or spirit, a hunter brought down his prey or a healer drove away the negative forces causing illness. Just as the presence of an animal's footprints could lead a hunter to the presence of the animal, so too arose the belief that a symbol could bring about the manifestation of the very thing it symbolized. This principle was one of the earliest forms of magickal thinking.

The ancients saw within Nature the workings of Divine Consciousness. In other words, just as we can look at a painting and say this is the work of Rembrandt or Van Gogh, so too the ancients discerned the *techniques* of divinity within the ways of Nature itself. Study focused upon the lesser life forms because the ancients believed them to reflect the basic nature of divinity. Such a belief also extended to rocks and gems. This is why we find the association of crystals, plants, and animals within occult symbols and correspondences. The magickal people of old devoted a great deal of study to them, realizing that divinity is most understandable through recognition of its handiwork.

In early tribal life, certain individuals were known for their ability to understand and use these methods of magickal thought. Whether we call them Shamans, Medicine Men or Medicine Women, or village Witches, theirs was an ancient

Craft. Just as the primitive tribes of our ancestors valued members who could shape pottery, make a bow, or fashion a spear, so too did they value those skilled in the craft of magickal practices. In time these people established a body of initiates from which evolved the priests and priestesses of the Old Ways.

Wicca, as the Old Craft, is a religion that teaches connections to Nature and more importantly to the forces behind Nature. Its purpose is, in part, to align an individual with the flow of energy on this plane and to teach rapport with deity. Participating in the seasonal rites attunes a person to Nature's vibration. From this arises an increase in *psychic* abilities. If you have ever been around animals in the wild, you can tell they are sensing things well beyond what their five senses reveal to them. It becomes the same for us when we share the *religion of Nature* with these untamed creatures.

By seeking an understanding of divinity within the ways of Nature we establish an unspoken communication with the Creators. As we come to know the Old Ways, we encounter and embrace the polarities of the *Great Spirit* (Goddess and God). Out of this we develop a reverence for them and establish a rapport. Every ripple of energy causes a response, whether that energy is in the form of a prayer or a ritual. In essence, the Craft is a system of learning how to work with these ripples. This is the art or "craft" of our magick.

The Craft is a system of spiritual development as well. It teaches us to walk in balance. We learn that everything connects and shares a relationship with everything else. What we do to the Earth, and to each other, we do to ourselves. The Old Ways teach reverence for life and the indwelling spirit, helping prepare us to someday dwell within the spiritual realms that await us, once we are free from the Cycle of Rebirth here in the physical dimension.

The Old Ways teach alignment and this extends to how we function as both physical and spiritual Beings within the world of Nature. Alignment also means becoming of the same vibration or frequency. Like attracts like in a metaphysical sense. From the perspective of the Old Craft, celebrating the seasonal rites bathes one in the energy tides of Nature. Through this union we become like Nature, meaning we attain a harmonious resonance with Her Ways. To attain such a vibration joins us with all that is natural and free (undeveloped and untamed). In this sense we are then of the same spirituality as a soaring hawk, or a beautiful bounding stag. In effect, we share the same religion or spirituality through this connection.

We see in Nature that deity is the one creator and maintainer of all that is. In an attempt to perceive it and communicate with it, we personify it as a goddess and a god. The God and Goddess of Wiccan theology are essentially opposite aspects or polarities of the Divine-Source-of-All-Things. In other words, they are those aspects of divinity which we can isolate as active and receptive, electrical and magnetic, masculine and feminine, etc. Look at all the names of gods and goddesses employed over countless generations, and you will see the many ways in which humankind has tried to connect in an intimate way with divinity.

There is much debate in modern Wicca as to what deity is, how we relate to it, and how we are part of it. In ancient times deities were personal gods and goddesses, perceived as beings who were conscious of us, caring and providing for our needs. With the influence of Eastern Mysticism (as interpreted by Western minds) some modern Wiccans view the gods as aspects of our Higher Selves, our own divine nature dwelling at the core of our being. In either case our relationship with what we perceive as deity is just that—a relationship. It carries with it some responsibilities and some degree of accountability, just as any relationship does. The debate here is where, and to whom, do such things pertain.

In the study of divinity as expressed within physical Nature, the ancients chose animals reflecting corresponding aspects of divine expression. An object or living creature was chosen because in some concrete fashion it displayed to the human mind something of its own character that reflected a spiritual principle in a physical manner. Therefore the traditional sacred animals of gods and goddesses, and the prescribed magickal plants and stones of Occultism, have all been passed down through generations as examples of the generative and germinative powers of divinity as expressed within Nature.

Within the ancient Mystery Traditions, priests and priestesses dressed themselves in animal disguises, wearing masks and the fur or feather coverings of various animals in order to symbolize divine principles and natures. They did this also in an attempt to align themselves with the spiritual current flowing through the creatures it animated. To become the animal was to become the principle, and to become the principle was also to become its source. This is a very important aspect of magickal reasoning. Out of such magickal thought among ancient secret societies arose the concept of such mythological creatures as the centaur, satyr, harpie, and unicorn.

Enough remains from ancient sources concerning the ancient Mystery Traditions in the Aegean and Mediterranean regions (Old Europe) to have preserved many of the ancient Mystery Teachings. Ancient Egypt, a Mediterranean nation, preserved the Old Way concepts in the images of their gods. Many early Egyptian deities are portrayed with various bird heads. Among Neolithic religious icons discovered in Old Europe we find that carvings of bird deities preceded humanoid deities and most other animal forms as well. The Greeks and Romans also possessed very advanced Mystery Cults such as the Eleusinian Tradition and the Cult of Dionysus.

In the mythology of northern Europe we find many of the same Mystery themes. In Teutonic lands we see Odin (who gained enlightenment by hanging from a tree) and his ravens, along with Loki and the wolf. In Celtic lands we find Epona and the horse, Cernunnos depicted with a stag, and Blodeuwedd with her owl. In the Tale of Taliesin many bird and animal forms appear as symbols of the powers of divine transformation. The Goddess in this story ends up swallowing the God who has transformed himself into a seed. The seed impregnates the Goddess and she gives birth to a renowned bard known as Taliesin. A study of this mythical legend reveals the inner mechanics of divine transformation as it moves through the physical dimension, planting the seed that can become enlightenment within human consciousness— *the seed of spirit born in the womb of matter.*

The Ancient Agricultural Mysteries

Plants are an integral key to understanding the Old Ways. Our ancestors attached symbolism to different plant parts, such as flowers or leaves, because of what their shape resembled, or even what the nature of the environment in which they grew suggested. Often something of their physical nature indicated magickal powers, such as the sunflower always turning to face the sun, or the moon flower only opening its petals at night. Here they symbolize many abstract principles and therefore we find them included in the mythology of ancient gods and goddesses. Other reasons for including plants as occult symbols are related to what we now term their pharmaceutical or chemical natures.

Occult symbolism appears in the act of the seed pushing its way up through the soil. The plant grows from a seed, flowers, produces seed, and dies; so too is the life of a man or woman. The beauty of the flower is fleeting in its time, just as youth itself soon departs, and the life of the plant lives in accord with the seasons of Nature. Plants that did not die in the Winter were believed by our ancestors to have particularly strong magickal powers. For this reason, evergreen trees were themselves worshiped as deities in the ancient times of our ancestors.

Tree worship was widespread throughout the ancient world. Groves of trees served as the first places of deity worship. A tree was rooted in the Earth and stretched upward, extending its branches into the sky. Trees provided shelter and food for living things and our ancestors highly revered them as spiritual Beings. The Oak tree was sacred to many cultures, particularly to the Druids and Celts. In southern Europe the walnut tree was worshiped as sacred to Diana, Hecate, and Persephone. The Scandinavian world-tree known as Yggdrasil symbolized the supporting structure of the nine spheres of Teutonic cosmology. In Hebrew mysticism, the magickal and philosophical system known as the Kabbalah is based upon a tree design.

Ancient sorcerers, magicians, and prophets carried staffs or wands made from sacred trees as a sign they were emissaries of the gods. Later such sacred objects came to be viewed as vessels of magickal power wielded by the magician. From the view that plants were magickal arose the tradition of carrying roots such as the mandrake or pouches filled with special herbs as a means of transporting the power of various plants. Making wreaths with sacred plants was an attempt to draw the power of the associated deity, enclosed in a ring which symbolized its cycle in the Wheel of the Year. To wear such a wreath denoted that person as a Divine King, one who represented the deity here on the Earth.

The magickal staff of Dionysus was a giant fennel stalk capped with a pine cone. He typified the Divine Kings who became the slain gods of European paganism so common throughout all of Europe. Essentially, the concept of the slain god is that the vital essence of the deity dwelling within the human vessel is buried in the earth to renew the fertility of the land. The ancients understood that life sprang forth from the seed, and that seed came forth from the plant at the height of its vitality. To control that vitality one had to harvest the plant. From this basic Pagan concept arose the custom of slaying the Divine King.

Over time, the slaying of human beings evolved into the killing of animals associated with the cult of a particular god or goddess. The discovery of thousands of Paleolithic and Neolithic icons is clear evidence that the earliest forms of worship focused on animals. These ancient animal gods and goddesses eventually evolved into cult animals associated with a humanoid deity such as Athena and her owl, Oden and his ravens, and so on. As people matured in religious and spiritual expression, ancient human sacrifice was replaced by animal sacrifice.

Animal sacrifice evolved into plant sacrifice as the hunter-gatherer society became an agricultural society. In the case of Dionysus, his blood was the wine from the grape and his body was the vine. The Divine King became the Harvest Lord, killed at the time of his ripened grain. He is known by many names, such as the Green Man, John-Barley-Corn, Haxey Hood, or Jack-in-the-Green. The ever-repeating theme of this concept is "renewal." This renewal restores divine energy not only to the soil to replace what the crops have consumed, but also to the lives of the people. By consuming the Divine King before the passing of his prime, each individual came away with their own inner natures revitalized.

In many cases the sacrificial body is burned and the ashes scattered on the Earth. In agricultural societies the ashes were scattered over plowed fields to ensure the fertility of the soil. (An old European custom still practiced in some places is to burn effigies of mythical figures at the closing of the year.) It is important to note the magickal associations of burning an effigy connected to agriculture. Heat and light are essential to the growth of a plant and to its production of fruit or grain. The fire represents the sun light and moon light that first gave birth to the agricultural deity. Just as the plant goes to seed and dies, only to produce another plant, so too does the god die so that he may live again. Therefore, the Harvest Lord returned to his source, completing the Cycle of All Things. In a Nature religion, how could it be seen any other way?

Magickal links and the nature of subcultures to retain inner symbolism have created many important cultural traditions. It is quite common in Europe today to see the remnants of Pagan worship displayed in agricultural themes. The Harvest Queen, or *Kern Baby*, is one example. In this tradition the last sheaf of the harvest is bundled by the reapers, who proclaim "We have the Kern!" The sheaf is then dressed in a white frock decorated with colorful ribbons depicting Spring, and hung upon a pole (a phallic fertility symbol). This is the survival of the Corn Spirit or Corn Mother described by Frazer in his book *The Golden Bough*[1] (see chapter two for "Corn Mother").

In Scotland the last sheaf of the harvest, called the "Maiden," must be cut by the youngest female in attendance. If the harvest is not completed by Samhain (Hallowmas), then the last sheaf is called *Cailleach* or "Old Woman." Just as the Kern Baby was hung upon a pole, the Cailleach (also known as *Kylack*) is traditionally hung in the barn. When the first grains have been ground into meal, a portion is placed in a barrel and mixed with ale and whiskey. Farmers invited to the Meal and Ale celebration all partake of their fill. Once in a thoroughly festive mood the farmers go into the barn and dance beneath the Kylack. This type of celebration is traceable to the ancient Roman Harvest Festival where celebrants danced beneath effigies of Ceres, the goddess of grain.

Secrets of Ancestral Memory

The Old Ways speak of connectivity to the Source-of-All-Things. They teach that Divinity is reflected in Nature, and Nature is reflected in the diversity of life-forms within it. The Old Ways reveal that Nature is the Great Teacher. The higher principles of Divinity appear within Nature through a reflection of the ways of Spirit. The Creators established the Laws of Nature so that through them we might come to know the Laws of Spirit. When we observe the ways of Nature around us, we see that everything has purpose and reason. Even what we as humans see as cruelty in Nature is only a reflection of the duality in all things. In ancient wisdom the gods were

---

1 Frazer, James George. *The Golden Bough; A Study in Magic and Religion* (New York: MacMillan Company, 1972), pp. 471–478.

feared as well as they were loved. In the old Mystery Tradition teachings, what humans saw as tragedy the gods saw as a play.

Nature teaches all living things what they must know in order to survive and flourish. Imprinted within them is the knowledge that teaches birds to make their nests, animals to hunt and survive, humans to crawl and walk. This is what those who study animal behavior call the *innate releasing mechanism* (IRM). In his book *Primitive Mythology,*[2] Joseph Campbell describes this principle when he tells the story of the sea turtles.

Hundreds of sea turtles are born at a particular time in the sands just above the tide line. On the very day they are born huge flocks of sea gulls circle overhead picking them off as the tiny turtles literally race to the water. What is interesting here is that the newborn turtles already know in which direction the water lies, that they have to get to it quickly, and they already know how to swim when they first enter the water. They have no previous knowledge of any of these things, since they have never experienced them before, yet they are clearly driven by something within them to get into the water as rapidly as possible.

In another study of animal behavior mentioned by Campbell is the account of how newly born chicks will dart for cover when the shadow of a hawk passes near them, but they do not do so when the shadow is that of a duck, pigeon, or the like. Campbell calls this *the image of the inherited enemy* and says that this image lies sleeping in the nerves awaiting the proper stimulus to evoke it. Here we brush up against not only the "collective consciousness" described by Carl Jung, but also against the metaphysical principles of the supernatural world wherein lies the hidden secrets of the divine mechanism.

Human beings also possess innate response mechanisms (IRM) but are much more influenced by central excitatory mechanisms (CEM) than are other animals. CEM refers mainly to a person's reaction to such things as endocrine gland secretions (as in testosterone and estrogen) and external stimulation

---

2 Campbell, Joseph. *Primitive Mythology* (New York: Akana, 1991), pp. 30–35.

by such expressive outward signs as aggression or seduction. As Campbell notes, instinctive behavior in humans is more open to learning and conditioning than it appears to be among other animals. In humans, individual experience can alter instinctive reactions to a much larger degree than is demonstrated by other terrestrial life-forms. Therefore we must use caution when applying the IRM or CEM principles to our own species.

What is fascinating, and relevant to the theme of this chapter, is that the ancient gods themselves are stimulating signs to the IRM within humankind. Ancient rituals were designed as catalysts to the internal mechanisms within human beings, serving to transform the mundane nature into the divine. Humans are, in a metaphysical sense, a microcosm within the macrocosm of Nature. Men and women created various rites that expressed not only their needs, but also caused some higher power to respond to those needs. This is why ancient Mystery Traditions passed on secret rituals from generation to generation. Therefore we may look at rituals of antiquity as a set of catalysts stimulating the innate response mechanisms that lie asleep among the sensory nerves of the human spine.

The ancient myths of goddesses and gods are records of how divine energies can act and react when viewed from a human perspective. They symbolize the interaction between human and divine consciousness. This is one of the reasons why care should be taken when reconstructing traditions and choosing deities for one's system of practice in modern Wicca. As Campbell points out, myths are not rational accounts and cannot be understood from a rational approach. He goes on to say that it is "ridiculous" to try to interpret them in a theological sense, and that to analyze them from a literary perspective reduces them to metaphors. Campbell concludes that the most fruitful approach to interpreting myths is to study them as stimulants to IRMs.

While I do not entirely agree with Campbell's views on the irrelevancy of theological elements within mythology, I do feel that his general words of caution are wise. In *Primitive Mythology* he speaks of the various approaches to mythology, categorizing them into historical and nonhistorical. Campbell notes that the religious experience is psychological and not dependent upon the circumstances of human history per se. On the other hand it is the factual circumstances underlying the myths that help us to interpret them. Campbell likens the cultural/ethnic elements to a magnetic field that draws everything together. It is important to understand that mythical images are not independent of the actual world that they reflect. Therefore, they are not independent from the culture in which they arose. This is true even though many mythical images and themes appear to be almost universal among the ancient peoples of the Earth.

The mythology of the Old Ways is very simplistic on the surface, but contains layer after layer of hidden symbolism. Essentially the myths establish a goddess and a god who preside over Nature and all within it. The Goddess of Wicca is a mother goddess associated with the Moon and traceable back to the Neolithic cult of the Great Goddess. The God is the Lord of Animals, associated with the sun and also traceable to Neolithic, if not Paleolithic, times. Nature is viewed as animated by a host of beings personified by such things as fairies, nymphs, satyrs, and other magickal creatures who vitalize Nature with their energy. They are, in effect, the *inner mechanism* of Nature from an occult perspective.

The Old Ways view Nature as the spiritual blueprint for creation. By studying the formulas and designs of Nature, one can discern something of the inner workings of the *mind* that created it. This is why there is such a close emphasis on working with Nature Spirits and Elementals in Wiccan Magick. Ritual circles are traditionally cast by evoking Elemental Beings to help empower the rites. Offerings are frequently left for them, especially at the Summer Solstice and at Samhain. This is because both ritual seasons are associated with fairies and spirits of the departed. If you are interested in further study, my book *The Wiccan Mysteries*[3] contains a great deal of information linking fairies with the Neolithic Cult of the Dead.

Connected with the Wiccan teachings concerning the God and Goddess and Nature spirits we also find beliefs related to power animals or spirit guides. As humans gained an ever-increasing awareness of themselves, a tendency arose to focus more upon improving the qualities of mundane life than upon studying the ways of Nature. The Magickal Craft users accordingly created links through the animal world to keep a bridge established between civilization and Nature. As noted earlier, various animals reflected aspects of Divine Nature emanating from Physical Nature. By creating spiritual links with the spirits of Nature, men and women could maintain a link to Nature through their rapport with the indwelling spirits of various animals. This is where spirit guides come into the picture. The Old Ways teach that we are not totally self-directed, as in "the blind leading the blind." Nor are we carried along like a log in the currents of a river. We are guided by things conscious and greater than ourselves, but we have the freedom to make our own choices. The trick is learning to listen to our guides and to our own intuition, balancing both the external and the internal.

Although we cannot realistically say that humankind lost its connection with Nature, I think we can say that we have collectively stopped listening and responding to Her. The ancients spoke with Nature as a storm was brewing, performing rites and leaving offerings. Modern humans more frequently pile up sandbags and secure shutters, viewing natural forces as the enemy. The Old Ways teach us that we are part of Nature and Her cycles. When we walk with Nature we flourish, and when we move against Her, we put ourselves in peril. Animals live by Her laws and they remind us of Her Ways. They help us recall that we too are Nature's children.

---

3 Grimassi, Raven. *The Wiccan Mysteries: Ancient Origins and Teachings* (St. Paul: Llewellyn Publications, 1997), pp. 186–187, 269–270.

The following chapters are rooted in the view of the Old Ways as presented here. It is important to understand that the mentality of the Old Ways is still relevant and essential to the modern Craft. The Old Ways are the very soul of Wicca. If we can blend our modern intellectual views with the ancient feelings preserved by the Old Ways, we can grow into an even more powerful understanding of Wiccan Magick. As with all things, we must seek to walk our path with balance.

Chapter Two

Folk Magick
in Wicca

*What we see as essential to Folk Magick
is the art of imitation or mimicry—
what we call sympathetic magick. Our
Pagan ancestors believed that the forces
of Nature could be attracted and directed
by personifying the principles of Nature
through ritual enactments.*

Folk Magick is the belief in supernatural forces inherent in natural objects, as well as a belief in various types of spirits. Unlike ceremonial ritual magick, the structure of Folk Magick is very simplistic. Often there is no apparent reason for the production of the magickal effect within the spell or charm (or related to any of its required ingredients). Please note that I say that there is no "apparent" reason for the magickal effects of most Folk Magick spells. There are indeed several reasons why this type of magick is practical and effective. In this chapter we will examine the hidden and obscure reasons underlying this form of magick.

In chapter one we examined old European concepts of Nature and magick. The intimate relationship between our ancestors and Nature is a legacy handed down in the Folk Magick tradition. If it is accurate to say that Wiccans possess a faith, then this faith would be the belief in mystical connections. Pre-Christian European religion left us a very rich heritage of magickal and mystical belief. To the early peoples, the universe appeared controlled by a host of spirits and deities. Humans, as users of tools, soon assembled objects believed to have influence over those entities that inhabited the unseen world. Most pagans were very poor common folk and had little access to the type of tools associated today with Wicca and Witchcraft.

The ritual tools now associated with Wicca are the pentacle, wand, blade, and chalice. One of the earliest examples of these tools appearing together in a magickal context is found in the Tarot card of the Magician. The earliest depiction of a Magician with these four specific tools is found in the Cary-Yale Visconti deck (see page 181). This Italian deck was created during the fifteenth century for the Visconti, a noble Milanese family. Tarot cards later spread to France and throughout Europe. Playing cards had appeared a century earlier in Spain and then in other European nations (mentioned in bans against gambling and vice in general) but these were not Tarot cards. It is doubtful that the average European peasant possessed either Tarot cards or ritual tools of such nature during this time in history.

Instead our ancestors depended upon herbs and magickal charms to protect them against spirits or to enlist their aid as necessary. Fairies and other Nature spirits possessed a duality and were neither entirely good nor evil. Care had to be taken not to offend these spirits or to trespass upon their sacred places. In fact the earliest mention of fairies of any kind in England occurs in the *Anglo-Saxon Chronicles* (circa A.D. 800) addressing charms against *elf-shot*. Gustav Henningsen's writings on the Sicilian fairy faith are of particular interest. In them we find evidence of a sect composed mainly of women (*The Ladies from the Outside*[1]) who could heal people inflicted by fairy magick. They also knew the proper offerings to leave to appease the fairies. Unlike our ancestors, most people of New Age philosophy view fairies as totally benevolent beings. In Old Europe, fairies were both good and bad.

Hermetic Influences

The Renaissance, originating in Italy, recovered a great deal of occult knowledge accumulated during the classical Greek and Roman periods. During the Middle Ages Hebrew magick became mixed with Hellenic, Roman, Egyptian, and Persian/Chaldean teachings. The Roman Catholic Church opposed the occult revival during the Renaissance. Many respected writers of the period such as Ficino, Campanella, and Pico openly defended magickal philosophy as a natural science. Ficino and Pico taught that Nature can be manipulated through an understanding of magickal correspondences found in Nature. Campanella believed that magick was a science in and of itself.

In Italy, during the early part of the Renaissance, many ancient Greek and Hebrew texts were translated into Latin and Italian. *The Key of Solomon* (*Clavicula Salomonis*) appears to have first been translated into Latin, followed by an Italian and then French translation. *The Book of the Sacred Magic of Abra Melin the Mage* first appears as a French translation of the Hebrew text. Many magickal texts appeared in southern Europe during the Renaissance—as early as the fourteenth century, and expanding greatly by the fifteenth century. By the sixteenth century many Latin, Italian, and French works appear in English translations in northern Europe. One of the earliest and perhaps most profound works based upon older texts was *Occult Philosophy of Magic* written by Cornelius

---

1   Ankarloo, Bengt, and Henningsen, Gustav, editors. *Early Modern European Witchcraft; Centres and Peripheries* (London: Clarendon Press, 1993), pp. 190–215.

Agrippa in 1533. His English translation was published in England in 1651.[2] Translations of older Hermetic texts later influenced English occultists such as John Dee, Robert Fludd, and a host of others.

You may be wondering what all this has to do with Folk Magick in the Wiccan Tradition. The answer is quite simple. A great deal of Gardnerian Wicca has its roots in the *Key of Solomon* which displays the ritual tools and various symbols used by Gerald Gardner. Agrippa's book, along with *The Magus* by Francis Barrett (1801), contains many of the Folk Magick associations typical of Wicca during the 1950s and 1960s. The vast majority of magickal concepts known today originated from what was preserved by Renaissance manuscripts, but to understand the role of European Folk Magick in Wicca as a Mystery Religion we need only look to the simple peasant farmers and their Pagan lore.

The Harvest Lord

The advent of agriculture helped develop a strong connection in magickal thought between an object, an act, and a result. The seed is the object, planting is the act, and crops are the result. In addition to this another magickal concept arose, that of *timing*. There is a time to plow, to plant, and a time to nurture and harvest. Long ago Nature became the blueprint by which Folk Magick systems operated and evolved. Before anyone knew what was contained within the seed it was simply an object of power. Our ancestors simply thought that a spirit dwelled within the seed and that this spirit would produce the plant if treated appropriately.

Ancient people viewed the plant itself as a manifestation of the spirit that once dwelled within the seed. When harvest time came, the plant spirit was believed to flee from bundle

---

2   For a more recent edition of this work, see Llewellyn Worldwide, Ltd.'s 1993 edition of Agrippa's *Three Books of Occult Philosophy*, edited and annotated by Donald Tyson.

to bundle as the harvest was stacked in the fields. The trick was to capture the spirit in the last bundle before it could escape the field totally. Then it could be returned to the soil, thus making the seeds planted in the Spring even more powerful. In early times, when a stranger appeared in the community at the time of the Harvest, he was seen as the plant spirit trying to sneak off in the guise of a human. To keep this from happening the stranger was seized and sacrificed in the last sheaf upon the harvest field. His blood spilled back into the soil, returning the fertile spirit.

In modern times this practice is now symbolic. There are still cases in which a visitor to a farm community during the time of harvest is captured and harassed by the locals. Often this person is tied up and held for a time—all in good sport, or so say the locals. When no strangers appear at harvest time, the last reaper in the field becomes (and became) the Plant Spirit and is subjected to the same treatment. This is because the Plant Spirit, driven out by the cutting of the last sheaf, must now take on another form. Therefore he passes into the reaper, who becomes the embodiment of the spirit.

Folk Magick also retains the ancient teachings of an obviously matriarchal era. When the wind is passing through the fields of grain, peasant farmers often say, "Here comes the Corn Mother" or "The Corn Mother is passing through the corn." Among ancient people, Her presence was believed to help make the crops grow and mature. The images of corn dolls at harvest time are a remnant of this ancient belief. In Old Europe a wreath was made from the last sheaf and was worn by a maiden until the festival season had passed. Then it was put away until Spring. Later the wreath was taken, mixed with the seeds from the last sheaf and buried in a newly plowed field. In Germanic lands the last sheaf was often called the Great Mother, Old Woman, Old Grandmother, or Harvest Mother. We see similar practices in Scotland as well, where the last sheaf is called the Maiden (or shorn Maiden), Witch, or Old Woman.

What we see as essential to Folk Magick is the art of imitation or mimic—what we call sympathetic magick. Our Pagan ancestors believed that the forces of Nature could be attracted and directed by personifying the principles of Nature through ritual enactments. In the drama play, the participants evoked a secret mystical influence through sympathetic magick, hoping to encourage the spirits to take up the drama in their own realm and thus produce the desired results on Earth. This is another illustration of the occult phrase: *as above, so below.* Folk Magick rituals are, in effect, an attempt through imitation to encourage Nature to initiate the wheel of the year in a timely and fruitful fashion.

In Folk Magick the symbols and objects themselves are believed to possess power. They remind the spirits of the principles behind the object, the act, and the result. For example, seeing that the dinner table is being set means that supper is about to be served. The symbols of the plates, utensils, and cups evoke a sensation of hunger and anticipation. The manifestation of food being served is assured by the presence of the symbols. So too it is with Folk Magick principles.

Inner Workings of Folk Magick

To someone experienced in ceremonial/ritual magick, a Folk Magick spell may seem empty and lacking in power. Folk Magick usually lacks the more complex structure of ceremonial and ritual magic. The connections to its source of empowerment are not always clear. Therefore some people may dismiss these little works of magic as too simplistic or as simply unfounded superstitions. Even today, there is a great deal of Folk Magick employed by eclectic Wiccans, much of it comprising entire magickal systems. There are several reasons why these folk practices have continued and can still be found in use today.

When Folk Magick spells do work, they work for one of four reasons. First, they work through suggestion—also known as sympathy (assuming that the person believes in either the spell itself or in the person who gave them the spell). Second, they work through the actual physical properties of the objects themselves (such as the chemical nature of the herb) or through their etheric properties (such as the indwelling *mana* or *numen*). Third, the spells work through the association of some spirit or deity with the objects involved in the spell (the most common reason in days of old). Fourth, and something skeptics would claim, is that they work through coincidence or through basic dumb luck, like the flip of a coin. Unfortunately there are times when an individual passes on to someone else a spell that he or she has never performed. Instead, they have copied it from somewhere, or heard of it from somewhere else. It's likely that whoever it was borrowed from obtained it from someone else in the same manner. This is one of the ways in which nonsense is kept alive in a tradition and passed along down through the years.

To those who invest the time, however, a great deal of eso-teric knowledge can be obtained from a study of Folk Magick. Ritual magick involves the employment of metaphysical laws and/or the assistance of deities or spirits of some type. This is sometimes referred to as "formula magick." Formula magick does not concern itself with unrelated fragments of folklore or with superstitious belief. It is based upon supernatural laws (the etheric mechanism behind the forces of nature) and the laws of physics. Hidden within the fragments of Folk Magick are the keys to actual magickal power. One of the secrets here is what occultists call atavistic resurgence, and another is what Wiccans call "the well-worn path."

What this all means is simply that some things are so deeply rooted in the "group consciousness" of a community that they generate a response without the performer even knowing anything about them. On a mundane level, let's consider the "power" of an obscene gesture such as extending the middle finger at someone. If you had someone from a different culture (who did not know its meaning in America) display this gesture in any American city, the response would be unquestionable and immediate. It would still evoke the associated response because it is part of America's *Group Mind*. It is a magickal gesture and instantly creates a change in another person's consciousness. It is independent of the user's own knowledge of it.

There are many examples of Folk Tradition still employed by people, even though they don't know the meanings. When someone sneezes we usually say "bless you"; when someone spills salt he or she may toss a pinch over their shoulder. Often someone will say "knock on wood" when they are speaking of their good luck so far. All of these have ancient Pagan origins and some are connected with old beliefs concerning ancient spirits. To "knock on wood" was to thank the spirits of the forest who were believed to bestow good fortune upon humans. To forget to thank them was considered an insult and might cause them to withdraw their good will, thus their role in one's good fortune was remembered by knocking upon something made of wood. To sneeze was to risk expelling the soul, therefore a blessing was spoken to anchor the life spirit. A person spilling salt addressed the presence of an evil or mischievous spirit, which had a natural aversion to the purity of salt. To toss the salt over the shoulder banished the spirit who hid behind the person so as not to be noticed.

Many modern tools and symbols continue to retain their ancient connections and can still evoke their once time-honored responses. The old spirits can still be stirred by the ancient calls and gestures, if performed with traditional techniques. Witches, Pagans, and Wiccans have continued to perform them since the days of antiquity—the connections have never been lost or severed. There is a certain amount of power inherent in Folk Magick items, simply from momentum alone.

When employing the Folk Magick tools and paraphernalia of Folk Lore you are using living connections with the Spirits of Old. The Elders say that there never has been a time when the old rites have not been performed, nor has there been a time when the ancient offerings to gods and spirits have not been placed for them. One of my teachers once told me that if the Old Ways were to disappear, then the spirits of Nature would withdraw from humankind. The sun and moon would no longer rise, the seasons would not return, and the world would wither and die, but as long as one Wiccan practices the Old Ways all will be as it was in the time of our beginning.

When Folk Magick Doesn't Work

Now we must look at the down side of using Folk Magick in modern times. If some of the Folk Magick techniques you employ bring no results, then you will want to give this section of the chapter some reflective thought. In this eclectic modern age portions of Folk Magick practices are gathered together from various regions in Europe that are culturally unrelated or disconnected. Therefore it is difficult to produce much in the way of any consistent magickal effects because the occult associations have never evolved as a cohesive tradition within the cultural group consciousness.

Often fragments of early Pagan belief appear in books on magick but have little if any influence over anything other than our imaginations. One of the most common misunderstandings today concerning the art of Folk Magick stems from the difference between magickal formula and Folk Magick belief. To better understand the differences (as well as the fallacies) let us take a look at how Folk Magick originated.

In the early villages of humankind were found the local shaman or Witch who was the healer and performer of magick. This person was knowledgeable and experienced concerning the properties of plants, the use of natural energy, and the ways of the supernatural. The majority of people in the local community were busy with hunting, farming, and the concerns of everyday life. They had little time to spend on the things that the local Witch was mastering. When someone needed the services of the village Witch, they simply sought him or her out and requested assistance.

The Witch would usually gather some herbs and charms together, magickally charge them for the desired purpose, and give them to the person with a set of instructions. This person might be told that he or she should place the charm under a pillow, or wear it in a bag upon the body. They might be told to place the herb in their shoe, or some other place. What they were not told was how the object was prepared and charged beforehand, or how its magick worked. Only the Witch knew these secrets, as they were part of his or her art. This resulted in the person believing that all one had to do was to obtain that particular herb and place it in a shoe, and the desired effect would take place. This person would then go off and tell another, who would tell another, and so on. Thus the misunderstanding grew and became a Folk Magick tradition. If the desired results were acquired following the use of the herb or charm, that was great (and so grew the reputation), if not it was attributed to personal lack of power or "evil" spirits.

Using the local village Witch as an example, let's take a look at the difference between her or his magick and Folk Magick. The Witch would have prepared a plot of soil in which to raise a collection of magickal plants. Sometimes this would be in a field or forest, or in her or his own private garden. The proper phase of the moon would be considered, as well as the season of the year. The seeds would be blessed, usually in the name of a deity or spirit, and planted in the soil. Laying his or her palms on the soil, the Witch would then "pass energy" into the buried seeds, often visualizing the plant at the peak of its growth. Once the sprouts appeared, the Witch would then begin an almost daily visit to the plants, speaking to them and passing along visual images of the properties which he or she wished the plant to possess. This served to "charge" the plant with magickal properties that could be drawn upon at a later time.

Physical charms were prepared in a similar manner, passing mental images into the material itself. Typically this would be performed at the time of the full moon, as energy is most effectively channeled and condensed at this time. The Witch would also do the same with oils which were prepared in the prescribed manner, again at the time of the full moon. Oils are effective because they can retain a magickal charge. They can be charged when you are "at your best" and used later when you need healing, or when you need to draw upon energy levels that you do not possess at the time. With these items, the Witch had at his or her disposal a variety of energy forms to draw upon for magickal manifestations.

Mental images, in a magickal sense, are what we refer to as *thought-forms*. In other words, they are thoughts which are condensed through concentration, and then directed into an object for storage. The human brain generates electrical energy, and its etheric properties are the vehicle through which this process takes place. Breath is also employed as a directional energy and is referred to in ancient grimoires as "a vapor" or "a vaporous magick." Add to this vapor an emotional release, and you can transmit quite an effective charge when combined with mental imagery.

I believe that it is easy to see how employing these aspects toward a magickal goal is going to be a lot more effective than simply sticking a sprig of an herb under your pillow while you sleep. What serves to complicate the issue of Folk Magick versus Formula Magick is that Folk Magick is curious and interesting. What we need to remember is that Folk Magick, in many cases, is simply a collection of fragmented spells and Pagan concepts. The actual spell behind these fragments was part of a secret art and was kept from the populace. Rarely does Folk Magick contain the esoteric aspects of spell working and the results can be inconsistent. In many cases all that remains of a once intact ritual are the related fragments of an herb here or a charm there. Author and Folklorist Charles Leland summed this up quite correctly in his book *Etruscan Magic and Occult Remedies* where he wrote the following passage.

We find the ancient continually confirming the extreme antiquity of the modern. Be it a tract here, a small observance there, now an herb in an incantation, and anon a couplet in a charm, they continually interlace, cross, touch, and coincide. I find these unobserved small identities continually manifesting themselves, and they form a chain of intrinsic evidence which is as valuable to a truly critical scholar as any historical or directly traditional confirmation.[3]

What Leland addresses here is that these fragments all indicate the antiquity of a former tradition. They may be likened to the bones of a dinosaur; they represent the original form, but are singularly not the same thing, nor do they possess the same vitality of their former status. Still, Folk Magick curiously persists and is kept alive in many traditions. Let us all keep in mind that merely because something is ancient does not necessarily mean it is wise or correct. The same is true of anything contemporary. There is as much ancient folly as there is ancient wisdom. The bottom line is that you should examine a spell and consider whether there is any reason it would work. What is its goal and what steps does it take to accomplish that goal? What source of power does it draw upon and how does it connect with that power?

Spells don't work just because they are spells; there has to be a reason. A rhyme has no power in and of itself, nor does a pile of dead plant material purchased in an Occult Shop. These things are simply catalysts and components that assist us in our magickal consciousness. Look for a formula if you want to find a practical spell or work of magick. Discern what the source of its power or influence is (is it you, a spirit, a deity or what?). If there isn't any source of power then there isn't any power.

---

3 Charles Leland. *Etruscan Magic and Occult Remedies* (New York: University Books, 1963).

Chapter Three

The Herbal Craft

The ancients taught that prayers or requests were carried on the smoke of the incense. What better way to be heard by the gods than to send your words upward on the scent of their favorite plant.

We cannot speak of Wiccan magick without addressing the use of herbs in rituals, spells, and works of healing. The village Wiccan has long been the local pharmacist, dispensing herbal potions to those in need. He or she has also been the diviner, counselor, and the provider of magickal charms and amulets. In this one person we can find the doctor, therapist, and priest or priestess of our ancestors.

Our Pagan ancestors believed the gods gave us the herbs of the fields in order to provide cures for both physical and spiritual ailments. In addition, some of the gods gave us certain herbs to help us deal with spirits and forces outside the material world. Essentially the gods saw the need for the herbs before the need was manifest in the Physical Plane. Our ancestors developed a system of associating these herbs with stars and planets. The power of the herb is derived from its astral connection.

In primitive thinking our ancestors believed that herbs contained an indwelling power called a numen. The numen was the divine creative spark dwelling within the creation, and therefore it had a consciousness of its own. Over the course of time this concept shifted to thinking of the power within a plant as mana, and later still as a Nature Spirit such as a fairy. This is one of the reasons the ancients devised specific methods for harvesting herbs. The spirit within the herb had to be treated with respect in order to harvest its magick. One such method required that the herb be cut with a single slice from a knife on the night of the full moon.

There are four basic aspects of the Herbal Craft: *planting, caring, harvesting,* and *employing.* These four steps are the occult mechanisms linking the Wiccan to the indwelling spirit of the herb, and helping to empower it. By using this formula the Wiccan can enter into a magickal relationship with the plant, and thus gain the favor of its spirit so that it will lend its aid to a work of magick. When we examine each of the inner aspects in this chapter we will come to a better understanding of herbal magick.

Planting

To begin you will first need to prepare a plot of soil in which to raise a collection of magical herbs. You can use a planter box or a flowerpot if space is limited. Traditionally the herbal garden would have been secretly prepared in a field or forest, or surrounding the local village Wiccan's hut. The proper phase of the moon should be considered, as well as the season of the year. The new moon is the best time to plant seeds or transfer sprouts because the moon is waxing, meaning that its powers are growing and increasing. The seeds should be blessed using the name of a deity or spirit with which you have rapport, or one that is associated with the nature of the type of magick you have in mind for your herbal garden.

Once the soil is ready for planting, place the seeds in the palm of your hand and pass energy into them. Do this by slowly taking in deep breaths and slowly exhaling the air out three times upon the seeds. Then bury the seeds and place both palms over the soil and again perform the breathing charge. This time you will also visualize the plant at the peak of its growth, so make sure you know what the mature plant will look like. Water the seeded area a little each day with pure water, not tap water. Do not drench the soil, but do keep it moist. If you are using packaged seeds check the instructions.

There are many good herbal books available and you should become familiar with the needs of the various herbs you desire to grow. The traditional magickal associations of herbs are important because they reflect the herbal knowledge of our ancestors. I advise that you stick to the traditional magickal correspondences when working with any herb. Once you have some experience then you can begin to experiment, but in the beginning it is wise to draw upon the time-proven methods of those who practiced long before us.

The Care of Herbs

Once the sprouts appear, begin an almost daily visit to them. Speak to them as the conscious beings they are; ask them how they are doing, tell them how beautiful they look and encourage them to grow. They will not understand your spoken words but they will understand the intent of your energy. Sit with them for a few moments each day and pass to them visual images of the properties which you wish the plant to possess. This serves to *charge* the plant with magical properties that can be drawn upon at a later time. This is an important stage because you are directing the magickal images and currents at this time.

Mental images are what I refer to as *thought-forms* in chapters five and seven. Essentially they are *thoughts* that are *condensed* through concentration and then directed into an object for *storage*. The human brain generates electrical energy and its etheric properties are the vehicle through which this process takes place. Breath is also employed as a directional energy and is referred to in ancient grimoires as a *vapor* or a *vaporous magick*. Add to this vapor an emotional release and you can transmit quite an effective charge when combined with mental imagery.

Remember to care for the physical needs of your herbs. This is part of establishing a good rapport with them and of gaining their favor so that they will aid you in your magickal arts. Some herbs require more or less water than do others, so consult a good herbal book. Generally speaking, all herbs require good drainage so it is wise to have gravel or sand beneath the soil. I have provided a list of recommended reading in the back of this book.

Harvesting

There are time-honored techniques to harvesting herbs, many of which are based on the principles of Moon magick. Even without deferring to tradition it is important that the Wiccan go about the business of collecting herbs with a very clear reverence. If the act of gathering the herb does not mean enough to you to perform the extra steps, then you've lost a certain portion of magickal power before you even start. Mentality is the primary tool of a Wiccan's magick, and if you do not weave an air of magick, then you are simply performing a mundane task and nothing more. You must be fully present in every act of magick, or in any step connected to it. The Wiccan statement of *"and as my will so mote it be"* is a declaration that your magick is as strong as your will. If you give little effort then you take little power.

In traditional herbal magick there are nine steps to gathering herbs. First the herb must always be taken with the left hand. This is because the left hand is receptive. When the power of an herb is harvested it is received and not taken. Second, the wind (if any) must be at your back when the herb is gathered. This is because wind indicates the presence of spirits and to have them support you from behind is beneficial. To have them pushing against your movements is detrimental and you risk offending them. In other words you are either with the flow or against the flow. Third, you must never look back over your shoulder. This is because you might scare off the fairy folk and other nature spirits who have gathered to take witness. Thus abandoned, you risk negative charges on the herb.

The fourth step in harvesting an herb is to trace a circle around the herb with your magickal blade. This prepares the spirit of the herb for withdrawing and ensures that it stays with the herb when harvested. It is essential that iron never come in contact with the herb or touch inside the circle at any time. Iron negates magickal magnetic charges. The fifth step requires that you speak to the herb, telling it why you need its help and what you are about to do to it. The sixth step is to place the herb in a pouch, never letting it touch the soil. If it touches the soil the spirit will pass back into the soil. This is not unlike the principle of the harvest lord discussed elsewhere in this book.

The seventh step is to wear no jewelry or clothing and to have abstained from sexual intercourse for seven days (a lunar quarter). This helps to magnetize your aura, and being nude while you gather the herb makes you a creature of Nature again, free from the signs of domestication. The eighth step is to leave a small gift or offering in the hole from where the herb was withdrawn. The traditional offering is a mixture of equal parts of wine, honey, and milk. In place of this, a silver or copper coin may be planted as a gift to the Earth spirit. Perhaps the best offering might well be a new herbal seed. The ninth and final step is to kiss your hand to the moon as a token of love and respect.

When taking an herb in this manner you will want to decide in advance whether you need the entire plant or simply a leaf or two. The leaves will only provide you with pharmaceutical ingredients, as would only the roots or stems. To obtain the spirit of the plant you must harvest the entire plant intact. Calculate your needs accordingly and take the necessary steps. If you harvest only the leaves of an herb then avoid pouring the libation directly upon the plant. If using a coin simply press it into the soil nearby.

Magickal Use of Herbs

Our ancestors started with the seed and worked with the plant as it grew. The plant was established and raised as a type of *familiar spirit*. This is the numen or spirit which I spoke of earlier. It is the divine spark of the creators within their creations. Numen can be amplified within an object through magick, and the numen spirit can be contacted and enlisted in the art of spell casting. This relationship is the reason ancient Grimoires were very specific concerning the planting and harvesting of magickal herbs.

Once dealt with properly, the power of the numen can be carried along in the various parts of the plant, empowering the herb. The ancients also taught a table of correspondences as shown on page 215. In the art of magick it is clear that there are energy imprints left within the electromagnetic make-up of all living organisms. These imprints are caused by emanations from the moon and the planets of our solar system. Plants such as the Sunflower and the Moonflower were given associations to planetary bodies because they physically change position as they "follow" the sunlight or moonlight with a turning of their flowers. Other plants were associated with Venus due to their heart-shaped leaves, to Mars due to their fiery chemical natures (peppers, tobacco, etc.), and so on.

Herbs are also employed for their natural pharmaceutical properties in magick and ritual. Some induce magickal states of consciousness, either through ingestion or inhalation, and this can aid in the casting of spells, or in other works of magick. Transformation of one's consciousness, by whatever means, is essential to the art of magick. I must add here that drugs are not absolutely necessary and that changes of consciousness can be adequately attained through meditation and personal will power.

Preparing Your Tools

Physical charms and amulets can be charged with magickal consciousness, passing mental images into the material itself, just as was done with the herbal seeds. This would usually be performed at the time of the full moon as energy is most effectively channeled and condensed at this time. The same holds true of oils prepared in the prescribed manner, again at the time of the full moon. Oils are effective because they so nicely retain a magical charge and can be charged when you are at your best. Later, when you require healing, or need to draw upon energy levels which you do not possess at the time, you will have at your disposal a variety of collected energy forms from which to draw for magical manifestations.

Herbs, in the form of incense, potions, charms, etc., can be used to bless ritual tools and to enhance their power. One technique is called *loading* the tools. This involves placing certain herbs inside a ritual tool, typically candles or the ritual wand. You would hollow out the bottom of the candles about an inch or so deep with a hot metal probe, gently pushing and twisting it into the candle. Then pack the herbs into the hole and seal them over with melted wax. For the wand simply hollow out the shaft, or if you desire you can hollow the head of the wand and then glue it back in place. Herbs can then be packed inside the wand, along with a crystal or power stone if you wish. A list of herbs and their magickal properties is given at the end of this chapter.

Another technique involves brewing an herbal potion in which a ritual tool may be bathed. Prepare the potions by boiling some purified water and steeping the appropriate herbs in the water for about twenty minutes. Then the ritual tool may be placed in the potion. Depending on your needs, you may wish to use several different potions for each tool. You may also consider adding elemental condensers for an additional charge (see chapter five).

A good potion, useful for purifying or re-consecrating a tool, is made of equal parts of: vervain, basil, woodruff, hyssop, and myrrh. Add a pinch of salt to boiled water and then add the herbs. Allow them to steep for twenty minutes, then bathe the tool in the mixture after the water has cooled a bit. Afterward rinse the tool off with fresh water. To add additional potency to any charge use equal parts of periwinkle, Solomon's Seal, and mandrake. Place the herbs in the pan and place a lodestone in with them. Allow the herbs to steep for twenty minutes in boiled water and then plunge the tool into the mixture three times. If you are charging an athame or metal amulet you will find it effective to heat the metal before plunging it into the herbal potion. The reaction of the water and the hot metal will add an extra charge. Rinse the tool off with clear water after you have finished.

For a general blessing of any ritual tool, use equal parts of pennyroyal, rosemary, hyssop, and acacia. Steep for twenty minutes and then strain the liquid through three layers of cheesecloth. Add the filtered herbal liquid to another bowl half filled with pure spring water. Then float a few freshly picked roses on the water. Wait five minutes and then bathe the ritual tool. Rinse with fresh water afterward. If you prefer instead to cense the tool with herbal smoke you can pass it through the smoke of herbs burning on a charcoal block.

Magickal Associations

Generally when considering any plant for magical use you must break it down into symbolic aspects. Its coloring, habitat, fragrance, taste, peculiarities, and chemical properties are all important to correspondences. It is necessary to understand the elemental associations as well. The root is Earth, the stem is Water, the leaves are Air, and the flower is Fire. Fragrance is considered to be the fifth element of Spirit.

Determining any correspondence for a plant to a zodiac sign, planet, or whatever will relate to the part of the plant used. This in turn relates to the symbolism considered in the previous paragraph. The Moonflower plant is a good example of the mixed symbolism of plants. Its leaves are heart-shaped which, together with their green color, links the plant to Venus. Its flower is white and opens only after sunset, which links it to the moon. If it bears thorns, this would show a Mars influence. The seeds of the Moonflower are hallucinogenic, making it a truly shamanistic plant. Most powerful magical plants have either trance-inducing or hallucinogenic properties.

Plants, like stones, possess a numen or spirit consciousness. They are not singularly as "powerful" as stones, but they are more versatile and can be used in more varied ways. In magick the plant (or more properly its Numen) is employed to gain in the performance of spells or rituals. The plant can be used as an incense, or an ingredient in an oil, or to empower a potion. The plant can also be used as a familiar, which is an older and less known aspect of plant magick.

Various herbs were associated with a certain goddess, god, or spirit. These herbs were then offered up as incense to "attract" the deity or spirit to the work at hand. The ancients taught that prayers or requests were carried on the smoke of the incense. What better way to be heard by the gods than to send your words upward on the scent of their favorite plant. Traditionally herbs were added to the bonfires that burned at Solstice and Equinox. These time-honored herbs were: fennel, rue, thyme, chervil seed, geranium, and pennyroyal.

Plants also became associated with the gods or with mythic heroes or heroines through their appearance in the myths. In most cases the plant somehow resembled the nature of the character in the myth, and later came to represent that character in ritual settings. This is typical of various grains, evergreens, and so forth—all having something of the nature of the goddess, god, or spirit concerned. Certain grains appear in various meals, and do have connections with old Witch Lore. A blessing of the Sabbat meal that I use addresses this:

> *Blessings upon this meal, which is as our own body. For without this, we ourselves would perish from this world. Blessings upon the grain, who as seed went into the earth where deep secrets hide. And there did dance with the elements, and spring forth as flowered plant, concealing secrets strange. When you were in the ear of grain, spirits of the field came to cast their light upon you, and aid you in your growth....thus through you I shall be touched by that same Race, and the mysteries hidden within you, I shall obtain, even unto the last of these grains....*

The Witches' Broom

Traditionally a Witch's broomstick was composed of three different plant materials. The handle was made of ash, the sweep was made of birch twigs, and the binding to the handle was made of willow strips. Ash gave the Witch power over storms, birch provided protection from evil spirits, and the willow bound the Witch to the service of her goddess Hecate Triformis. The broomstick was made of three materials and thus was a triad symbol itself.

The broom can also be viewed as the duality of male and female polarities, the handle being a phallus symbol and the broom representing female genitalia. Some covens make a ritual broom to serve as such a symbol. Placed at the north quarter of the ritual circle, it represents the divine couple in their place of power. The ritual broom can also be used to sweep the circle prior to laying it out. When the circle is cut or opened so that someone may enter or exit during a ritual, the broom can be laid across the opening as a temporary barrier. In some traditions the broom is a tool of banishment and by sweeping toward the door, or swatting through the air, unwanted spirits can be chased off.

The Herbs of Witchcraft

Although there are hundreds of herbs used in the art of herbal magick, I have collected here the names and attributes of a few that have a particular reputation of mystical and magickal associations.. As indicated, certain of these herbs cannot be safely used. Please heed the warnings. A reading list for further information is also provided at the end of this book.

When considering the use of herbs for magickal purposes there are several ways in which the herbs may be incorporated. They may be burned as an incense, carried in a pouch, or hung as a talisman. The liquid forms are known as infusions, decoctions, tonics, and tinctures. An infusion is a specially prepared tea with the herbs steeped for five minutes in hot water. A decoction is similar, except that the herb is added to boiling water and simmered for ten to twenty minutes. A tonic is an herb steeped in wine. A tincture is an herb soaked in hard liquor. The herb is placed in a sealed jar with vodka or brandy, for example, and put aside for two weeks.

For Purification

Dragon's Blood	Mint
Myrrh	Pennyroyal
Vervain	

For Enhanced Potency

Dittany of Crete	Periwinkle
Pennyroyal	Mandrake
Solomon's Seal	

For Protection

Cinquefoil	Rue
Dragon's Blood	St. John's Wort
Fennel	

For General Blessing

Acacia	Orris root
Hyssop	Rosemary
Moonflower	

For Matters of Love

Balm of Gilead	Lovage
Coriander	Laurel

Magickal Associations

Balm of Gilead *(Commiphora opobalsamum)*

This herb was used in ancient times as a very special gift of love. Balm of Gilead has a very tranquil effect and when mixed with red wine is said to be very seductive. It is a good mixture to use for uniting new coven members with present members following initiation. Used as a decoction: one to two fluid ounces. Used as a fluid extract: one half to one drachm.

Belladonna *(Atropa belladonna)*

The plant named for the beautiful lady, belladonna is poisonous. It was used in what might be considered some of the darker magickal arts. It was also used to induce a trance for astral projection. [Dosage withheld, this is too dangerous for experimentation.]

Camphor *(Cinnamomum camphora)*

This herb is sacred to the moon and is the main ingredient in most lunar incenses. Inhaling camphor fumes from essential oil stimulates the intellectual centers in the brain and has a calming effect upon the psyche. It is an excellent scent to inhale prior to beginning divinatory practices. Camphor extracts are available in most pharmacies. Used as *Spirit of Camphor:* five to twenty drops. As a tincture: one half to one drachm.

Cinquefoil *(Potentilla reptans)*

This herb has a reputation in love spells and divinatory practices to discover one's true love. Cinquefoil is one of the herbs listed in the so-called Witches' Ointment, along with smallage and wolf's bane, mixed with wheat and animal fat. Used as a fluid extract: one half to two drachms.

Damiana *(Turnera aphrodisiaca)*

This herb has a stimulating influence upon the reproductive organs. Mixed with coffee liqueur, it is said to be an aphrodisiac. Used as a fluid extract: one half to one drachm.

Dittany of Crete *(Dictamus origanoides)*

This herb has a reputation as an enhancing herb in invocational incense. Mixed with sandalwood, benzoin, and vanilla bean, it is burned for astral workings. As a bulk herb: one half to one ounce dried leaves.

Dragon's Blood *(Daemonorops draco)*

Also known as Dragon's Blood Reed, this is one of the best herbs to use against negative energy and black magick. It can be ingested as a protection against psychic or magickal attack: two drachms added to red wine during attacks or when going to sleep.

Eyebright *(Euphrasia officinalis)*

This herb has a reputation for increasing psychic perception. Used as a psychic tonic: one ounce of dried leaves mixed with equal parts of goldenseal and fennel (quarter ounce).

Fennel *(Foeniculum vulgare)*

This is a protection herb and a counter to black magick. Mixed with St. John's Wort on Midsummer's Eve it was used to banish evil. Giant stalks of fennel were fitted with sprigs of rue by Italian Witches who fought ritual battles for an abundant harvest during the Ember days of the sixteenth and seventeenth century. Used as an oil: five to ten drops. The seeds may be burned in incense for protection as well.

Foxglove *(Digitalis purpurea)*

Associated with love spells, this herb is actually the source of the heart medicine known as digitalis. Legend has it that this ingredient was once part of a love spell recipe sold to liquor manufacturers in Italy. It is now a popular drink there called *Strega Liquore.* [Dosage withheld as this is a dangerous plant.]

Mugwort *(Artemisia vulgaris)*

This plant is also known as St. John's plant (not to be confused with St. John's Wort). It has an occult reputation for increasing psychic abilities and for prophetic dreaming when stuffed into a pillow. Used as a fluid extract: one half to one drachm.

Myrtle *(Myrtus communis)*

This plant is sacred to the Fairies and is used in Fairy spells and magick. Grown in or near a magickal herb garden, it is said to attract Nature spirits to take up residence in the garden. Used as a bulk incense.

Pennyroyal *(Mentha pulegium)*

One of the most powerful herbs to use in an oil of Initiation. It has a long-standing occult tradition for activating the higher nature and has a very strong spiritual vibration. Used as an essential oil: one to three drops.

Rue *(Ruta graveolens)*

The name of this herb is derived from the Greek *reuo* which means to "set free." It was also known as the "Herb of Grace" and its branches were used as aspergillums to sprinkle Holy Water at High Masses during the Medieval period. In Italian Witchcraft, rue is associated with the Harvest Lord and is called "the bitter essence of the God." Magickally it is an herb of protection from the powers of Darkness. It is used as an essential oil: one to five drops.

St. John's Wort *(Hypericum perforatum)*

This is another herb of protection associated with fairy magick and Midsummer's Eve. Mixed with fennel and rue on this night, it is considered very potent magickally. It is used as a charm or burned as bulk incense.

Solomon's Seal *(Polygonatum officianle)*

This herb has an occult reputation for banishing evil spirits and protecting anyone in its presence from harm. Used as a bulk incense.

Verbena *(Lippia Citriodora)*

This herb has an occult reputation for cleansing and purifying. It is used as a decoction: three tablespoons.

Vervain *(Verbena officinalis)*

Ancients called this herb *Herba Veneris* because of the aphrodisiac qualities attributed to it. Priests used it for sacrifices; because of this practice the herb was called *Herba Sacra*. Verbena was the classical Roman name for altar plants in general, and for this species in particular. The Druids included it in their lustral water, and magicians and sorcerers employed it widely. In Celtic lore it is called the "Tresses of Taliesin."

Vervain is also one of the sacred herbs of Italian Witchcraft. It was one of the plants dedicated to the goddess Venus. She wore a crown of myrtle interwoven with Vervain. The

Italian witch charm known as the *Cimaruta* features a vervain blossom, symbolizing protection. The herb is also used as an offering to the Goddess and can be planted around shrines dedicated to her. When casting a circle for magical workings, vervain can be sprinkled along the perimeter of the circle for extra protection. Used as a fluid extract: one half to one drachm.

Vetivert *(Vertiversia zizaniodes)*

This herb has an occult reputation for breaking spells and hexes and is used in counter magick. Used as an oil: three drops. It may be used as a bulk incense.

Wolf's Bane *(Aconite napellus)*

This is a powerful lunar spell herb used in shapeshifting magick. It is also known as Monkshood. [Dosage is omitted as this is one of the deadliest plants known.]

Chapter Four

Mineral Magick

Common to many ancient cultures was the belief that spirits inhabited stones. Each stone possessed an individual spirit. It was believed that the aid of the spirit could be enlisted through various offerings to the stone spirit.

W hen we look at the history of humankind we can clearly discern the importance of the Mineral Kingdom in both a religious and magickal sense. This is evident from the primitive god and goddess icons of the Paleolithic and Neolithic Ages, the great standing stones of Britain, and the many dolmens, cairns, and menhirs of ancient Europe. The altars used by our ancestors were cut from stone and were revered as sacred objects. Stones, in the form of a grave marker or tomb, even marked the passing of a clan member from his or her tribe.

It may be that the earliest consideration of stones in a magickal context lies in the fact that sparks can be produced by striking two stones (such as flint) together. Fire was a mysterious force to our ancestors and the ability to evoke it from a stone must have made a powerful impression on the early human psyche. Such was the reverence of stones that early humans were known to have carried them from their original habitats when migrating. To possess a stone from one's homeland was perhaps to carry a connective talisman to the generative source of power. In human history, stones would later mark off boundaries and declare territories. Perhaps in this practice we are indeed seeing the memory of tribal stones symbolizing one's place in the scheme of things.

The carrying of stone talismans evolved over the centuries into the wearing of amulets and magickal rings. The pentagram symbol now associated with Wicca was the image etched on signet rings worn by the followers of Pythagoras. The number five figures prominently in Pythagorean philosophy and was incorporated into a star comprising the five Alpha letters from the Greek alphabet linked together at angles to one another (see illustration, below). The star symbolized the higher nature reflected in the lower nature.

The earliest-known Pythagorean ring originating from Crotona, Italy, circa 525 B.C.E., was pictured in the book *Imagini degli Dei degli Antichi* by V. Catari in 1647.

The Magickal Nature

According to the ancient Hermetic teachings of the European Mystery Tradition, the stars and planets radiate celestial energy into the crystalline forms found in the Mineral Kingdom. The crystallized energy within any given stone produces an astral virtue specific to the nature of the mineral form itself. From this the ancient Mystics established a table of correspondences connecting the stones with specific planets and specific powers. Today we associate, for example, iron with Mars, copper with Venus, lead with Saturn, quicksilver with Mercury, gold with the sun, and silver with the moon.

The belief in the inherent power dwelling within stones eventually led to seeing them as divinatory tools. A good example of this is the use of runic symbols carved on throwing stones. Another example is the use of a crystal ball in foretelling future events. In part this is connected to the belief that dwelling within the crystal itself is the divine spark of consciousness. This is known as its numen or mana, which connects it directly to the Source of All Things.

Everything that exists on the Physical Plane is an aspect of the Source of All Things. Physical objects are actually *solid* energy-forms existing in varying vibratory rates. The lower the vibration the more solid or gross the object appears to be. The Mineral Kingdom is the lowest vibratory rate of the Physical Plane. Therefore the energy-forms that we call rocks are the most dense forms we encounter as material beings. It is because of this vast concentration of energy that mineral objects appear in almost every magickal system.

Individual stones or gems within the Mineral Kingdom have their own vibration, influence, and occult function. These qualities can heal and vitalize when correctly applied. The nature of a stone acts to collect and condense higher vibratory energies focused upon it. The direct influence of any gem is on the aura of what it comes into contact with. In the case of human subjects, the aura is stimulated by the influence of the gem. The energy of the gem joins with that of the aura, creating a localized amplification of the merged energies. Depending on the stone, certain body chakras will draw the energy or respond in some manner.

The influence of most gems is very subtle and gradual. In most cases the gem must be used several times in repeated applications. It was for this reason that the ancient occultists devised a system of magickally *charging* gems to enhance their natural powers. This system incorporated the use of natural and artificial techniques. The following techniques are based on these ancient principles.

The Solar Charge

The Preparation

Place the desired gem in a pan of boiling salt water for about one minute. Remove the gem and dry it off completely, then place the stone under the noon sun for one hour.

The Charge

Make a tripod stand of dry twigs, preferably oak. Set the stand outside at sunrise with the gem nesting on top. Leave the stone in this position until 1 P.M. The stone is now charged with the sun's energy. Next, filter the sunlight onto the gem through a sheet of colored plastic or glass. The color of the plastic will be linked to the effect desired:

Red: This energy acts to vitalize and to energize. It has a stimulating influence on the genitals, although more on men than on women. When using red, charge the gem for one to two hours. When healing, work upon the subject for about a half hour, once a day. Recharge the gem every two weeks.

Green: This energy acts to soothe and restore. It works equally well on the physical and astral body. It is very useful for treating the eyes and the digestive organs. When using green, charge the gem for three hours. Work on the subject for one hour or more. Recharge the gem weekly.

Yellow: This energy is very stimulating, but in an "irritating" manner. It can stimulate the brain in moderate doses, but is normally used to fight infections, tumors, and so on. When using yellow, charge the gem for one hour. Work on the subject for three quarters of an hour. Recharge twice a month.

Blue: This energy acts to heal the energy fields, or auric bodies, of living organisms. It heals the material only through the non-material. The dark blues should be avoided as they tend to slow the healing process. Light blues are more preventive than they are healing. Medium blues are best. When using blue, charge the gem for three hours. Work on the subject for one hour or more. Recharge weekly.

Orange: This energy acts in a manner similar to red, but to a lesser degree. Its usual function is to stimulate the organism's natural healing system. It greatly increases the effectiveness of the internal systems. When using orange, charge for two hours. Work for one hour or more. Recharge weekly.

Violet: This energy acts in a very soothing manner. Its major influence is on the aura and affects the emotions in a positive manner. It is also mildly sexually stimulating to the female. When using violet, charge the gem for three hours. Work on the subject for one hour or more. Recharge weekly.

The Lunar Charge

This method is similar to that of the solar charge, with the following exception. Place the prepared gem under the moon at 9 P.M. or midnight. Leave it there for three hours. Then use the colored filter as in the solar method, but do this on the following night. This allows the magnetic energies of the moon to "set" individually within the gem. You will want to consider the phase of the moon, and the zodiac sign it "occupies." These energies will influence the work of the gem involved. This is the advantage of the lunar charge over the solar. The energy may not be as strong per charge, but the lunar charge is more diversified. Overall the lunar charge is more effective, although the solar charge works more quickly. Remember to avoid direct sunlight on a lunar-charged gem, as it will negate the charge.

The Magickal Charge

This method is used with either the solar or the lunar charges. While the filter is in place, the following technique is employed:

Place the tips of your index fingers and thumbs together, forming a triangle over the gem. Then visualize pure energy (as white light) forming within the triangle. Mentally impregnate the light with the qualities that you desire the gem to possess. Once this is completed, visualize the light passing from your hands to the gem. Mentally see the gem glowing. Finally, exhale three times on the gem through the triangle. If you wish to recite an enchantment then do so before this last step. You may wish to anoint the gem with a charged oil or condenser after all the charges are set. Anything that adds power is useful.

Rousing the Crystal

This is an ancient technique for evoking, or rousing, the power within a crystal. This method is best used on crystals, but any stone can be used by adapting it to the technique. At Lake Nemi and along the coast of Naples, Italian Witches known as *Strega* have long performed the following ritual.

On the night of the full moon wade out into a body of water until you are about waist deep in the water. If possible you should be nude. Seek out a spot where a rock is protruding through the water. If none is found then pick up a rock from the shallow water and carry it out with you.

Once you are prepared (standing out in the water) look up at the full moon and strike the crystal three times on the rock. Be careful not to damage the crystal as you strike the rock. You don't want to be too gentle or too rough. When performing this technique use the base or blunt end of the crystal. If you carried a rock out with you, drop it into the water where you stood once you had finished. This technique is best applied to awaken the *numen* (spirit/consciousness) within a newly obtained crystal, and then again later, to awaken any charges that you have set within it.

If you have a crystal set onto the head of a wand it can be roused with this method also. Another method used by Witches is to hold the crystal up to the full moon and then strike it three times with the wand. This would also be performed out in the water. If you desire, the appropriate crystals could also be roused beneath the sun. In this case you would not go out into the water, and noon would be the best time to perform the ritual. All other aspects would continue to apply.

According to ancient beliefs, all gems contained a magical stellar charge. Many stones were associated with stars and constellations. This system was the basis of the "birthstone" in astrological lore. The energy of the stars is condensed by the moon, and directed down on the Earth. This principle also applies to the energy of the planets. Many ancient grimoires contain material concerning stones, the stars, and planets. You may wish to consult a book written specifically on this subject for further information.

Common to many ancient cultures was the belief that spirits inhabited stones. Each stone possessed an individual spirit. It was believed that the aid of the spirit could be enlisted through various offerings to the stone spirit. The advantage of using stones magically was that stones seemingly lasted forever. The life force within a stone allows its material form to wear extremely well against the physical elements. Stones possess very strong spirits or numen. The numen is the "consciousness" of the gem.

The shape of the gemstone is also important for magical purposes. Gems that are pointed, such as the amethyst crystal, are transmitters of energy. Stones which tend to be rounded are collectors, excellent for establishing energy fields. This is very useful for the setting up of ritual circles (quarter stones). Pointed stones are excellent for spells that send their energy from one place to another. The ancient ritual circles were set with many small stones placed around the circumference. A crystal or pointed stone was set on the altar, marking the center.

Crescent-shaped stones were considered sacred to the moon and the Moon Goddess. The shape that a stone evolves into is caused by the nature of the indwelling numen. The physical elements that shape the stone are merely tools for the numen. Thus a stone shaped like a crescent could possess a spirit who could link the possessor to the forces of the moon. This stone would then be considered a charm or talisman. Stones are used for other purposes as well.

Healing with Stones

There are three techniques employed in the healing art of stones. These techniques may be used together or alone. The first technique involves the use of a wash or oil. Heat a pan of oil, or spring water, then pour it into a bowl. Condensers or other liquids may be added to the bowl to enhance the healing. The patient must be nude and reclining. The person performing the work should also be nude.

Take the required stone (for the healing energy needed) and dip it into the bowl. Beginning at the person's head (or animal's) rub the wet stone on the skin in a counter-clockwise circular motion. Visualize the area glowing with the appropriate color corresponding to the healing needed. Work downward along the body, making sure to work on each section of the body. You will need to re-dip the stone in the wash before moving to another area of the body. After dipping the stone, pause and visualize it glowing with the appropriate color.

After each healing is completed it is essential that you boil the stone in salt water for three minutes and recharge it. This will remove the negative energy which the stone has absorbed from the ill patient.

The second technique involves the use of a suspended crystal or stone. For this technique tie the gem to the end of a cord about twelve inches long. Beginning with the head, suspend the stone over the forehead. Swing the stone over the area in small counterclockwise circles. Visualize the same glow and color correspondences as in the first method. Move next to the throat area, then follow with the heart, solar plexus, stomach, and genitals.

The third technique involves the technique of *drawing out* with the stone. In this method you place the stone on the area of the body involved. Placing the right palm on the stone, begin a gentle kneading and drawing-out motion. Visualize a brownish or blackish color being drawn out into the stone. Do this as you rotate the gem in a counter-clockwise manner. From time to time hold the gem still, visualizing the appropriate healing color flowing from you and penetrating into the area of the body. Change back and forth between the two visualizations.

Whichever method you choose you should work slowly. It is wise to incorporate all three of these techniques in cases of serious illness. For prevention alone, one method will do. You may wish to have a friend or two work on the patient with you. This will save the healer from expending great amounts of energy.

Mineral Condensers and Elixirs

This simple method is used to charge a liquid substance with the properties of any given gem. These liquids could be ingested or applied externally, depending on the substance and its purpose. This method may be used alone or with the Magical Charge.

Amethyst

This is one of the most beneficial gems in existence. It has the ability to heal, purify, and to disperse negative energies. When used in an elixir or potion it helps to treat the blood system, heart, and lungs. Used externally, it nurtures the psychic centers and cleanses the aura.

The Method: Place the gem in a clear glass bottle. Fill the bottle with two parts spring water and one part of your favorite alcoholic drink. This alcohol should be fairly clear and at least 80 proof. Cover the bottle opening and leave it in the sun for at least six hours. Use once a day.

Moonstone

This stone acts more upon the inner being than upon the physical body, although as an elixir it does have the ability to heal ulcers, balance the endocrine system, and clear swollen lymph glands.

The Method: For physical treatments, use the same method as for the amethyst. In cases of ulcers you will want to use three parts water and one part alcoholic beverage.

For psychic or astral treatments place the gem under the moon for two nights, five hours the first night and four hours the second. The liquid mixture for this treatment should consist of equal parts of water and alcoholic beverage. You can add a magical condenser to this if desired.

Use this every night before going to sleep. The lunar-charged elixir is excellent for dreams, astral projection, and psychic development. In these cases you will anoint the appropriate centers and ingest the elixir. Investigate the properties of various gems for the preparation of other elixirs and condensers.

The Occult Nature of Stones

The following is a simple, brief listing of several stones commonly used for magical purposes.

Agate

The energy of this stone joins the heart and solar plexus together into a harmonious vibration. It also has a healing effect on the stomach. The energy of the agate serves to balance other energies and creates a stable, earthy energy field. Early Witches mixed crushed agate with water and herbs as an antidote for snake bites.

Amethyst

The energy of this stone has a general healing effect upon the physical and etheric bodies. When worn on a ring or necklace, the amethyst can charge the aura with the energy of spiritual love. Once its energy pattern is established within a person's aura, the stone serves as a protection against energies that are not harmonious to the bearer.

Early Romans believed that drinking from a chalice containing an amethyst would not cause drunkenness. Italian witches once taught that an amethyst bearing the sigils of the sun and moon would repel another's Witchcraft. (See Amethyst Quartz.)

Azurite

Aids in meditation.

Bloodstone

Stimulates the sexual energies of the base chakra. Once used by Witches in lust spells.

Carnelian

Another name for this stone is the Neophyte's Stone, as it serves to stimulate the inquiring mind, and moves one to activity. Early Witches used this stone as an amulet against "fascinations."

Chalcedony

Worn as an amulet, it will shield against energy directed against the wearer.

Chrysoprase

Being a variety of Chalcedony, it is similar in nature. Rather than being worn this stone is placed about the home for protection. One essential area is on the bedside table (or headboard).

Diamond

This gem has many associations in folklore. It was considered a symbol of truth and loyalty, and it was believed that the diamond would lose it luster if the owner broke an oath. Magically, the diamond serves to protect the bearer. It is especially protective for times when the conscious mind is unaware of the body (as in astral projection, coma, or surgery). It is said that the body cannot be "possessed" when a diamond protects it.

Emerald

Considered to be a transmitting agent for the emotion of love. The emerald exerts a positive influence on the heart physically and spiritually. Ancient magicians are said to have used this stone to see visions.

Jade

Aids in meditation. Red Jade serves to stimulate the emotions, green serves to calm. Jade has a general influence upon the inner motivations and urges.

Lodestone

Because of its magnetic attraction, many people associate it with the drawing of desired things. Yet reverse magnetism must be considered, and therefore it can repel as well. Some occultists color their lodestone in a symbolic manner in order to influence corresponding situations.

Moonstone

Aids in the development of the subconscious and psychic mind. In magic it draws the aid of the twenty-eight spirits of the moon and the favor of the Moon Goddess.

Quartz

Clear Quartz (rock crystal): Used as a focus for divination in spherical form (the crystal ball), and as a transmitter/receiver of energy. The magical link between the crystal and "other realms" is associated with magnetism, attraction, and accumulation in and around the crystal, by the infused iron throughout its structure. When charged by the moon's energy, the magnetic link is established. As the moon increases, so too does the generation, and accumulation, of lunar magnetism within the crystal.

Rose Quartz

Used to "lighten" the auric energy and to draw positive energy. Suspended over the heart area, the rose quartz filters and harmonizes energies passing through it in either direction.

Yellow Citrine

Considered a magical stone, it is used as an aid in the formulation of thought forms. Worn as a talisman during magical work, it stimulates the mind on all levels, and aids in the projection of "thoughts."

Tourmaline Quartz

Worn on the body, it aids in the projection of the astral form.

Amethyst Quartz

A powerful energizer, both physically and etherically. Aids in ritual magic by manipulation of the forces raised. In other words, it transmits energy directed toward it. Here it is best utilized by placing it on the center of an altar, or set onto the head of a wand.

Planetary Correspondences

Sun: Diamond, Topaz

Moon: Pearl, Opal, Moonstone, Clear Quartz

Venus: Emerald, Aquamarine, Rose Quartz,
Green Tourmaline

Mars: Ruby, Bloodstone

Saturn: Black Onyx, Black Jade

Jupiter: Amethyst

Mercury: Topaz, Chalcedony, Citrine

If you find a common stone that you desire to use in regard to a planetary charge, link it to the planet with a corresponding symbolic color. This is not completely accurate but may serve you well. Take into consideration the shape and location of the stone as well.

Planetary Influences Through Gem Stones

Sun: Vitalizes the blood and improves the circulation. Also benefits the heart and strengthens the mental will.

Moon: Stimulates the emotions and the subconscious mind. Influences body fluids and secretion.

Saturn: Balances disruptive energies. Causes a condensation of energy, sometimes known as organization.

Venus: Love and compassion. This energy establishes harmony between the heart and mind.

Mars: Aggression, force, motivation. Also influences the sexual energies.

Jupiter: Optimism, freedom, inspiration.

Mercury: This energy aids the mind in merging with other planes of existence. It also aids telepathy between beings. Influences the transmission of nerve signals.

Gems that Stimulate the Chakras

Crown: Amethyst, Diamond

Brow: Amethyst, Diamond, Jade, Opal, Clear Quartz

Throat: Topaz, Chalcedony, Citrine

Heart: Emerald, Rose Quartz, Ruby, Amber, Agate

Solar Plexus: Moonstone, Clear Quartz, Rose Quartz, Jade, Diamond, Agate

Spleen: Chrysoprase, Aquamarine, Citrine, Opal, Amber

Sacral: Amethyst, Jade, Moonstone, Opal, Pearl, Ruby, Diamond, Clear Quartz, Rose Quartz, Amber, Bloodstone

Zodiac Correspondences

Aries: Bloodstone, Diamond

Taurus: Sapphire, Jade

Gemini: Agate, Smoky Quartz

Cancer: Moonstone, Opal, Pearl

Leo: Ruby, Fire Agate

Virgo: Sardonyx, Carnelian

Libra: Sapphire

Scorpio: Aquamarine

Sagittarius: Topaz

Capricorn: Turquoise

Aquarius: Amethyst, Lapis Lazuli

Pisces: Moonstone, Aquamarine

Chapter Five

The Four
Elements

*The Elemental Plane connects to the
Physical Plane and it is through this
connection that Elemental activity helps
to renew the vitality within Nature.*

According to ancient teachings, creation was brought
about when the four basic Elements of *Earth, Air,
Fire,* and *Water* came together under the direction of
divine spirit. Many ancient myths speak of order coming out
of Chaos, the so-called taming of the Elements. In Wicca the
basic structure of physical and etheric material (the spiritual
essence) is believed to be composed of one or more of these
Elements. Earth is that property that binds and gives form.
Air is that property that liberates and stimulates. Fire is that
property that animates and activates. Water is that property

that makes things mutable and flexible. The physical representations of these four elements constitute their gross form in the material world.

Just as there is a duality in all things, the elements have what can be termed their *negative* aspect as well. In this context we may say that Earth is rigid, Air is flighty, Fire is destructive, and Water is stagnant. The Four Elements are kept in a positive and peaceful state through the mediation of Spirit, which can be called the fifth element. In Eastern Mysticism it is referred to as *Akasha*. The Wiccan pentacle (an upright five-pointed star) represents the four elements overseen and kept in balance by Spirit/Akasha (see illustration below). The Satanic pentacle, an inverted five-pointed star, represents the Four Elements dominating Spirit. It is important to understand that when we speak of the Four Elements we are speaking of types of energy. The physical forms of the Four Elements in the material world are manifestations of elemental principles and not the elements themselves

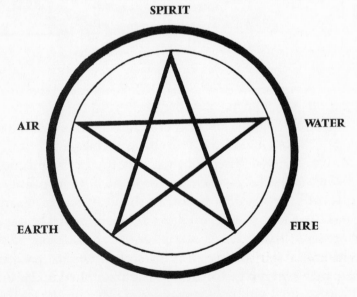

Elemental Pentagram.

According to ancient historians, Empedocles (a student of the teachings of Pythagoras) was the first person known to have taught the concept of the Four Elements as a single cohesive doctrine. He was also the first person to introduce the concept of the Four Elements into astrology, and their role in discerning the basic nature of the zodiac signs. Empedocles, who lived in Sicily, circa 475 B.C.E., presented the teachings concerning the Four Elements as the *fourfold root of all things*.

In European Occultism, these are the traditional assignments derived from the teachings of Empedocles:

Earth: Taurus, Virgo, Capricorn
Air: Gemini, Libra, Aquarius
Fire: Aries, Leo, Sagittarius
Water: Cancer, Scorpio, Pisces

Earth: cold + dry
Air: hot + moist
Fire: hot + dry
Water: cold + moist

In Roman mythology the four winds are deities with elemental natures. They are Boreas (north), Eurus (east), Notus (south), and Zephyrus (west). They are controlled by Aeolus, the deity who was the guardian of the winds, keeping them in order by chaining them. In this myth we see the Four Elements controlled by a fifth non-elemental power. This, of course, is the symbolism of the Wiccan pentagram.

Most Occultists credit Philippus Aureolus Paracelsus with what can be called the doctrine of the Four Elements. Paracelsus was an alchemist who taught that the four primary elements consisted of both a vaporous and a tangible substance. He believed that each element existed as both a physical element and a spiritual element. Paracelsus taught that just as there were two types of matter in Nature, a physical and etheric, so too must there be two types of Nature (the Physical

World and the Supernatural World). He further believed that within the Supernatural World there existed Beings native to each of the elemental regions therein. Thus Paracelsus assigned *Gnomes* to Earth, *Sylphs* to Air, *Salamanders* to Fire, and *Undines* to Water.

During the Middle Ages men and women were believed to have *composite natures,* meaning that they were a blend of spirit, mind, and body. Elemental Beings were considered to be creatures of a single nature related entirely to the property of their corresponding element. Just as fish are creatures of the water, and birds are creatures of the air, each Elemental is unique in form and function in a way that is appropriate to its elemental environment. Paracelsus taught that Elementals were invisible to human sight because they existed in a more subtle state than physical forms or phenomena. It was believed, however, that by condensing the etheric material of their forms, Elementals could appear in the physical world of Nature whenever they pleased. As Paracelsus stated it, the Elementals live in the interior elements while men and women live in the exterior elements.

The Elemental Plane

The Elemental Plane is directly connected to the Physical Plane and serves to empower, nourish, and animate the material world. One way to think of it is as a current of energy flowing through the earth, into the Astral Dimension, and then returning again to complete the circuit. In the river of Elemental energy are carried the thoughts and desires emanating from the Physical Dimension. In effect, the Elemental current delivers them to the Astral level, which in turn shapes what they symbolize into animated visual images. The energy of these Astral forms are then carried back to the Physical Dimension by the flow of Elemental energy into the material world.

The Elemental Plane connects to the Physical Plane and it is through this connection that Elemental activity helps to renew the vitality within Nature. In ancient myths we find many accounts in which humans and Nature spirits come into contact with one another and form various types of relationships. The ancient teachings tell us that the veil between the worlds was thinner then because humans had not yet developed enough to have a significant negative impact upon Nature. Therefore the vibrations within the natural world were more closely attuned to the Elemental Realms. The advent of the Iron Age signaled the eventual separation between the worlds.

Iron is the most effective magnet because its electrons do not oppose each other in their spin, which is what makes a metal magnetic. Therefore each iron atom is in effect a tiny magnet itself. Magnets have a tendency to align the atoms of other metals, thus making them magnets as well. A magnet produces a magnetic field that affects other electromagnetic fields. Elemental Beings have a polarity of their own allowing them to cross between the Physical Plane and their own Dimension. Iron is very disturbing to the energy fields of these beings and they have a natural aversion to it. In myth and legends fairies have a fear and a dread of iron—it is used against them in many ancient tales because iron can realign (or reverse) the fairies' electromagnetic polarity, making it difficult for them to return to their own environment. Lodestones (natural magnets) and iron amulets were favored tools against fairies and against magick in general for many centuries.

The Elementals

Gnomes

Gnomes are beings who inhabit the etheric elemental material of the earth's spiritual dimension. They possess a vibratory rate that makes them invisible to humans, but one that is still close enough to the lower physical vibration for them to interact with it. Their actions are reflected in the presence of mineral deposits, the erosion of rock, and the formation of crystals and other geological formations.

In ancient legends the Gnomes were protectors of secret treasures concealed in vast caverns beneath the earth. The old Sages taught that the Gnomes were not naturally inclined to aid humankind, but that if a person won their confidence and trust they would prove to be valuable allies. However, like all elementals, it was dangerous to deceive them or misuse their aid. Elementals work through the subjective nature of men and women, and can influence the human mind, bringing about gloom, melancholy, and despair. Conversely, they can also bestow confidence, steadfastness, and endurance.

The ancient teachings tell us that Gnomes are ruled by a king whose name is Gob. His followers came to be called Goblins as tales of them were told and retold over the centuries. They usually appear to humans as small, dwarf-like creatures.

Sylphs

Sylphs live in the etheric elemental substance of Air—within the spiritual medium of our atmosphere. Their activity is reflected in the gathering of clouds, the formation of snowflakes, and the growth and maturity of all plant life. In ancient times they were called the spirits of the wind, and were the source of many Greek myths and legends. Among the Elementals as a whole, sylphs are of the highest vibration and can thus traverse the dimensions more or less at will.

It is taught that the Sylphs have a ruler whose name is Paralda. Though essentially creatures of the air, sylphs reside on high mountain tops. Legend has it that they once spoke to humans through caverns and were the voices of ancient Oracles. It has even been suggested that the Muses of Greek Mythology were actually sylphs who had assumed human form in order to guide humans on a spiritual path.

Sylphs are associated with the activity of the human mind. They can influence and inspire humans; often they are said to gather around the poet or artist in order to impart their inner visions of spiritual beauty. They usually appear to humans in the classic fairy image.

Salamanders

Salamanders live in the etheric elemental substance of Nature's fire. It is through their activity that fire exists and can be used by humankind. Legend has it that fire Elementals were the first to befriend humans, teaching our ancestors how to make campfires. Ancient lore tells us that Salamanders are ruled by a king called Djin.

Salamanders move about most freely at night, appearing as balls of light drifting across various bodies of water. Old-time sailors often saw them investigating the sails of their ships— from this came the term *St. Elmo's fire,* describing the mysterious forks of flame that often appeared on old sailing vessels.

Salamanders have a profound effect on human nature since they are linked to the activity of our bodies through which we maintain a body temperature. They tend to influence our emotions and general temperament. When we say that someone is hot-blooded or a hothead, we are referring to their Elemental nature. Salamanders often appear to humans in the shape of small, lizard-like flames.

Undines

Undines live in the etheric elemental substance of humidity and within liquid natures in general. In ancient lore they are recalled in the images of water nymphs and mermaids. Springs, streams, and wells are favored by Undines. Their traditional abodes were among marsh reeds and vegetation growing alongside rivers and lakes.

Ancient lore tells us that the Undines are ruled by Necksa. They are friendly toward humans and their presence has a strong influence on our emotional well-being. The moodiness of an individual can be traced to their elemental nature. Just as water can be beautiful in a fall or river, it can also be unattractive in a stagnant pond. When we say that a person is all washed out, we are speaking of an Elemental influence.

The activity of Undines is responsible for the vitality within all liquids—therefore they play a vital role in plant, animal, and human life. Undines appear to humans most often in full human shape. Quite often the beautiful maidens associated with lakes and waterfalls in our mythology were Undines.

The Elements and Consciousness

Elemental energies can be drawn into the physical body and into the human consciousness for magickal purposes. One reason for doing this is to create a balance of Elemental natures within the psyche. According to Occult beliefs, positive and negative personality traits are attributed to Elemental conditions within the aura. The personality of the individual can be balanced by bringing the Elements into a proportional harmony. Traits related to vigor and vitality are associated with Fire. Those related to strength and endurance are connected to Earth. Traits associated with adaptability are linked to Water. Those of Air are related to creativity.

An imbalance of Elemental energies can result in one element dominating another, or in the opposite polarity of a specific element displaying itself. For example, a hyper nature can be viewed as either an overabundance of Fire or too little Earth. One method for determining someone's Elemental state is to make a list of personality traits. List all of the person's positive traits and negative traits. Then view each category and its relationship to the Four Elements. If there is an abundance of one correspondence and only a few of another, then one might be looking at an Elemental imbalance. This will provide a fairly accurate assessment of one's Elemental nature.

When working with elemental natures it is important to determine which elements are required to restore a balance. The rule of thumb here in the positive sense is: Water liberates Earth, Earth gives form to Water. Air gives life to Fire, Fire gives focus to Air. When too much of one Element is present it can be released by introducing its complimentary Element. The following is a sample list of positive and negative attributes.

EARTH	AIR	FIRE	WATER
+ Strength	+ Creative	+ Energetic	+ Adaptable
+ Endurance	+ Artistic	+ Motivated	+ Changeable
+ Steadfast	+ Intelligent	+ Dynamic	+ Compassionate
- Stubborn	- Flighty	- Combative	- Melancholy
- Lazy	- Distracted	- Destructive	- Pessimistic
- Dominating	- Paranoid	- Violent	- Stagnant

In a magickal context, each of the Elemental energies can be drawn and condensed within the human body for use as a personal power.

Magickal Uses of the Four Elements

There are four basic concepts that are useful in creating magickal influences related to the four Elements of Earth, Air, Fire, and Water. Both the astral and physical actions of the elements should be incorporated into a spell or other work of magick. Fire works through combustion, Water through mixture, Air through evaporation, and Earth through decomposition. These aspects not only empower and transform, they also connect one's spell to the forces of Nature and thus to the connected forces of the Supernatural as well. Generally, after spell casting or ritual work you will have some material left over to dispose of (wax, ashes, and so forth) and it is quite effective to use one of the Elemental methods to dispose of leftover material.

If your magick was intended to influence a situation, then the Earth Element is best employed. If it was to accomplish a specific goal, then Fire is a good source of motivation and energy. Romantic works are best connected with the Element of Water. Any matter concerning mental creativity or thoughts in general is best accomplished by employing the Element of Air. It is important to look at all of the aspects concerning the intended outcome. Break it down into Elemental qualities and employ something symbolic for each connective element. You will generally find that two or more Elements will be required to accomplish your magickal goal. The physical representation of an Element when working a spell is actually a focal point for accessing its astral counterpart.

The following examples will help you understand how to use an object associated with the appropriate Element:

Fire

Take a piece of paper or cloth and moisten it with three drops of the universal condenser described in the last section of this chapter. Place this in front of you and concentrate on the desired effect of your magick. Strongly imagine your thoughts to be pouring into the material, filling it with both your energy and Elemental energy. Imagine your desire being "written" by your thoughts across the material. When you sense that your concentration is breaking, then the material is fully saturated and you can stop focusing. Now simply burn the cloth or paper in an open fire. While it is burning, concentrate and visualize the end result of your desire. The fire releases the charge and merges it with the Element. The Element will then carry it into the astral level where it will take root.

Air

Take a small metal container and fill it about half full with clean water. Add three drops of universal condenser to the water. Put the container over a flame and concentrate on your desire as you gaze into the water. As the steam begins to rise, visualize what you desire. Once you have the image projected into the steam your desire is being drawn up and carried off. Continue concentrating on the desired outcome until all the water has evaporated.

Water

Take a container and fill it about half full with fresh water. Add three drops of universal condenser and three drops of rubbing alcohol. Now impregnate the water with your concentrated desire. As you do so, inhale very slowly and very deeply and then exhale out on the water's surface. Imagine your desire flowing out into the water. When you feel that the water is fully charged, pour it into a stream, river, or any moving body of water.

Earth

You may use either sand or garden soil. Ideally you will want to pick a spot connected to the desired outcome. If the spell is intended for a person then the soil should be somewhere that he or she will pass by on foot. If the spell is intended for a situation, you may want to sprinkle some of the soil in the setting. You may even consider potting a plant in the charged soil. In this way you can easily transport it to the target without anyone the wiser. The first step is to charge three drops of universal condenser added to a pint of mineral water. Concentrate on the desired outcome as you do so. Then pour out the mineral water over a selected spot of earth. This will allow the charge to be absorbed directly into the Element of Earth. Place both palms down upon the soil so that the index fingers and thumbs of both hands are touching the wet earth. Picture this as enclosing the area of wet soil between your hands. Conclude by performing the breathing charge as described for the Element of Water.

Elemental Condensers

Condensers are prepared fluids that are used to carry magical charges. One method of charging them is to place your hands together, palms down, so that the index fingertips meet as do the tips of the thumbs. If done properly you will form a triangle in the opening between your hands. Next inhale deeply, visualizing the full moon above your head. Bring the triangle opening in your hands over the condenser liquid and exhale three times through the opening and onto the liquid. As you do this, visualize the light of the moon pouring down through your head and into your lungs as you inhale and then visualize it flowing out with your breath as you exhale.

It is always wise to prepare bottles containing Elemental charges so that you have them when needed. Amber-colored bottles are best because they dilute the light entering through the glass. Sunlight will deplete astral charges and your magickal liquids are best kept away from it as much as possible. Also other types of colored glass tend to pass on the charge of the color itself, while amber is neutral and will not contaminate a pure or specific charge.

Once charged, an Elemental condenser can be used to empower a spell or ritual tool. Letters can be anointed with them to convey a specific feel. Statues can also be anointed with an Elemental charge for ritual work or spell casting. One example would be to take a fairy figurine and anoint it with an Air condenser. The statue can then be used to invoke a fairy spirit or simply to empower a fairy magick spell. Ritual tools can be charged with the Element they represent to add additional power. Traditionally the pentacle represents Earth, the wand is Air, the dagger represents Fire, and the chalice is Water.

Simple Condenser

This condenser can be used magically to stimulate one's psychic nature and to improve clairvoyance in general. To make this condenser take two level teaspoons each of camomile flowers and eyebright and place them in a bowl. Boil two cups of water on an open flame and then add the herbs. Set the mixture aside to cool for fifteen minutes. Then filter the mixture through four layers of clean linen cloth or cheesecloth.

For clairvoyance soak two cotton balls, close your eyes and place the balls on your closed eyelids for about twenty minutes. To increase occult sensitivity in the palms of your hands for the purpose of psychometry, place cotton pads on the palms of your hands for the same period of time. A simple condenser can also be drunk as a tea before employing a form of divination such as the Tarot cards or rune stones.

Universal Condenser

The purpose of this condenser is to accomplish magickal effects on not only the Material Plane, but also on the Mental and Astral levels simultaneously. Traditionally this compound is used to create artificial Elementals (serving spirits), to empower magick mirrors, and to animate paintings for use as portals or in meditation. This particular method uses the Moon Mansion charge in which the liquid is charged over a period of twenty-eight days, beginning with the moon in Aries. Check a good astrological calendar for this timing.

Take equal parts of the following ingredients:

> Angelica (Spirit)
> Tobacco (Earth)
> Mint (Air)
> Cinnamon (Fire)
> Watermelon (Water)

Add this mixture to a half quart of boiling water and boil for twenty minutes. Strain the water through cheesecloth. Pour the filtered water into a bowl and allow it to cool. Pour about two ounces of a *Frangelico Liquore* into a small bowl. Then suspend a piece of silver jewelry from a chain and heat it in an open flame until it is very hot. Next dip the jewelry into the bowl of liquor. If you made the jewelry hot enough you should hear it hiss as it enters the liquid. Remove the silver piece and add three drops of your own blood to the liquor. Finally, pour the liquor into an amber-colored bottle, add six ounces of water and cap the bottle. Place the bottle out at night using the Moon Mansion charge. A much lengthier and more powerful mixture is described in *Initiations to Hermetics*[1] by Franz Bardon.

Earth Condenser

Chop a small piece of parsley. Crush a pinch of caraway seed and add it to the parsley. Slice three petals from a carnation flower and mix all of this together. Then heat two ounces of olive oil and pour the mixture into it. Let it simmer for twenty minutes. Then strain the oil through a layer of cheesecloth and pour the filtered oil into a bottle. Add three drops of tincture of benzoin compound to it to keep the oil from spoiling. This tincture is available at most pharmacies. Label the prepared oil and charge it with the Element.

Air Condenser

Crush three juniper berries and three hazel nuts. Slice three rose petals and three leaves from a cherry tree. You can substitute the stems from a cherry if you cannot obtain the leaves. Prepare the oil as directed for the earth condenser. Pour the oil into a bottle, label it, and perform the Elemental charge.

Fire Condenser

Chop a very small amount (equal parts) of garlic and onion. Crush a pinch of mustard seeds and add this with a pinch of pepper to the garlic and onion. Add to prepared oil as described, bottle and charge the oil.

Water Condenser

Crush a small slice of a turnip and a sugarbeet. To this add three sliced peony blossoms along with three cherry-tree leaves (or cherry stems). Add to prepared oil as described, bottle, and charge it.

---

1   Bardon, Franz. *Initiations to Hermetics* (Wuppertal: Dieter Ruggeberg, 1971), pp. 195–199.

Using Elemental Energy

After spell casting or ritual magick you will have some material left over such as wax and ashes that you will need to dispose of in the proper manner. Each remnant will have an Elemental correspondence with which you can associate it. Then simply use one of the Elemental methods to complete the magickal process. The Earth Element will govern works associated with people and situations. Fire governs goal reaching and works of motivation, passion or destruction. The Water Element governs romantic and emotional works. Air governs matters concerning mental creativity and thought processes in general.

The following examples can be used to complete whatever spell you were working on.

Fire

Take a piece of paper or cloth and moisten it with the universal condenser. Place this in front of you and concentrate on the work of magic. Strongly imagine your thoughts to be filling the material. Imagine your desire being "written" by your thoughts across the material. When your concentration is breaking then the material is fully saturated. Now simply burn the cloth or paper in an open fire. While it is burning concentrate on your desire. The fire releases the charge and merges it with the Element.

Air

Take a small metal container and fill it about half full with water. Add three drops of universal condenser. Put the container over a flame and concentrate on your desire as you gaze into the water. As the steam begins to rise, imagine your desire being drawn up and carried off. Continue until all the water has been evaporated.

Water

Take a container and fill it about half full with fresh water. Add three drops of universal condenser and three drops of rubbing alcohol. Now impregnate the water with your concentrated desire. When you feel that it is full pour the water into a stream, river, or any moving body of water.

Earth

With this Element your concentration is centered on the universal condenser which you place in a jar after it has been loaded. This is then poured out over a selected spot of earth, to be absorbed directly into the Element of Earth.

Water Scrying

This technique is a very ancient one, and common among Shamanistic traditions. Divination is the ability to see what patterns are forming toward manifestation. What you "see" is actually what is likely to occur if nothing changes the pattern being woven. Here is a technique which I teach in beginning classes:

Pour some bottled water into a soup bowl. Mix either blue or a green food color into the water, so that the liquid is dark enough to obscure the bottom of the bowl. At this point you should have a reflective surface. Position two candles, as your source of light, so that the light does not reflect upon the liquid (off a foot or two, in front of you should do it). Next make a series of hand passes over the liquid, slowly and deliberately. Magically speaking, the right hand is of an electrical nature/active charge, and the left hand is of a magnetic/receptive charge. Right-handed passes will strengthen the image and left-handed passes will attract the image to form. Begin by making left-handed passes over the bowl, in a clockwise circle, just a few inches above the water (palms open and facing down). Stop and gaze into the dark liquid—not at the liquid, but into the liquid. You will need to repeat these passes occasionally as you work. Alternate between the left hand and the right hand. This requires patience and time. Use your intuition as you sit before the bowl. Make sure the area where you are working is quiet and there are no distractions.

Drinking some rosemary tea, prior to divination, can aid in the work. There are several herbs which aid the psychic mind—this is just one of them (be careful though, rosemary can be toxic in large quantities or with long-term use).

Chapter Six

The Astral Realm

*On the Astral Plane the etheric light
contains the blueprints on which the
material world is constructed. The
astral model that was imagined on the
Physical Plane is carried downward by
the Elemental Plane (or Plane of Forces)
into manifestation.*

According to Wiccan teachings, the Material Plane of existence has an etheric counterpart known as the Astral Plane. Just as physical matter is an accumulation and bonding of molecules, astral material is an accumulation and bonding of thoughts and concepts. What to the Physical Plane is a mountain, to the Astral Plane is a visualized concept. Everything created within the Physical Dimension was first a concept on the Astral Plane. This is why, in an Occult sense, we say that "thoughts are things." We also use the phrase "as above, so below" to denote the relationship between the various Planes of Existence (see glossary).

The Astral Plane is governed by two modes of Consciousness: the *Higher* Astral level and the *Lower* Astral level (although I will address a *Middle* level later in this chapter). The Higher level contains the emanations of divine thought, thus we can say that the arising astral forms from such an emanation create a natural *Being* within this Astral Dimension. The lower level contains emanations from the Physical Plane and therefore the resulting forms are not natural but artificial creations. By analogy we can say that human beings are natural creatures to the Earth, but the tools they create are not natural forms (cars, computers, and so on).

The ancient sages of Western Occultism called the lower astral level the *Terrestrial Dragon,* and the higher level they called the *Celestial Dragon.* The Terrestrial Dragon represented the forces of *Darkness,* and through its actions the negative astral forms were made manifest on the Earth. The Celestial Dragon represented the forces of *Light,* and through its actions were made manifest all that is beautiful upon the Earth (both physically and spiritually). The symbol of the Caduceus represents these twin serpents held in equilibrium by the wand. In this context the wand represents the middle astral level which separates and provides balance to the higher and lower levels.

The word "astral" is derived from the Latin *astrum,* meaning "stars." Astrum also refers to the heavens and to immortality. From a combination of ancient beliefs arose the concept of the Astral Plane or Dimension. The Inner Teachings tell us that there are two aspects (a duality) to everything: what something appears to be, and what something really is. In a metaphysical sense we say that everything is composed of form and force. A form is the manifestation of its force; the force dwells on the Astral Plane and its form dwells on the Physical Plane.

The astral force is composed of an etheric substance which we call *Astral Light.* It has magnetic and electrical properties expressed in metaphysical principles, and in the Physical

Dimension they are expressed in the principles of physics. The Astral Light forms around concepts, and here *thoughts* literally become *things.* On the Astral Plane, symbols are not ideas or concepts, they are manifested and animated forms. In other words, what is symbolic on the Physical Plane is tangible on the Astral. Likewise what is symbolized on the lower Astral Plane is material on the Physical Plane. An astral form is a living entity with an independent existence of its own.

The etheric material of the Astral Plane vibrates at a higher rate than does the material substance of the Physical Plane. Vibrations are so slow in the Physical Dimension that energy becomes dense, forming into gross material objects. On the Astral Plane the etheric light contains the blueprints on which the material world is constructed. The astral model that was imagined on the Physical Plane is carried downward by the Elemental Plane (or Plane of Forces) into manifestation.

In several places throughout this book I speak of the Elemental Plane being not unlike a river flowing back and forth between the Astral and Physical Planes. It carries the electromagnetic energy imprints of thoughts and desires arising within the material world and transports them off in its current to the Astral Dimension. The energy coming from the Physical Plane disturbs the etheric fields of the astral material. The Astral Light then shapes itself around the mental image and creates a form. If the vitality and structure of the thought is strong enough, then the astral form will survive and thrive. If not, as in the case of daydreams and idle wishes, the form will dissipate quickly and no physical manifestation will take place.

The magick of controlling this formula lies in one's ability to concentrate and project. When a person trained in mental discipline establishes a phantom image of that which is desired, he or she creates a link with the corresponding energies inherent on the Astral Plane. The emotional significance joins with the symbolism, which in turn attracts the astral substance, causing it to take on a shape. To ensure that the form survives long enough to become animated on the Astral level, one must pour emotional energy into a visualized form, sigil, or image related to the desire.

The ability of humans to *create* arises from the fact that we bear the divine spark within us of that which created us. In effect, we are a *Microcosm* of the greater *Macrocosm*. Our own inner nature contains the potential, although on a diminished scale, to wield the powers and forces of the greater divinity within us. When we invoke Elementals or Watchers, for example, we can do so because of the Macrocosm resonating within us. They respond to their own natures within us, as reflected in the Macrocosm of which they too are a part. When we cannot change the outer world around us we can turn to the creative source within us. If we can change the inner subjective world, then from the outer objective world will be drawn those things which we desire to manifest. This is the principle from which the old saying *"be careful what you wish for because it might come true"* originates.

Eliphas Levi spoke of Astral Light as an etheric substance being electromagnetic in nature. He said that it was the foundation upon which atoms came together to establish forms on the Physical Plane. He sometimes referred to Astral Light as the *Imagination of Nature,* meaning that consciousness dwelt within the astral material, directing the formation of thoughts and emotions into astral images. Such action is associated with the Lower level of the Astral Plane residing under the influence of the moon. On this level the process is automatic, whereas on the Higher Astral level (under the influence of the sun) the process is under the direction of celestial beings. An example of this higher nature is the formation of Egregores.

Egregores

Egregores are what some occultists call *divine thought-forms.* An egregore is composed of both human and divine energy joining together to create a *deity-form.* The formula for this creation can be seen in primitive worship dating as far back as Paleolithic times. A tribe carves an image of their deity and offers it rituals of worship with dancing, singing, and general forms of celebration. This energy impregnates the astral material, and an image forms within the etheric material of the Astral Dimension. At this stage of development the image is what we call a thought-form. In other words, it is energy formed into a mental image. If the ritual energy provided by the worshipers continues, then the thought-form becomes more cohesive. The thought-form begins to fix itself within the astral material rather than dissipating like a mist. Thus it adheres the Astral Light to itself and is empowered by Levi's "Imagination of Nature."

Divine consciousness dwelling within a higher dimension becomes aware of this formation due to the *ripple effect* or *domino effect* natural to the function of the Planes. Divinity responds to contact or communication whether in the form of a prayer or ritual. In response to the appearance of the image bathed in Astral Light, divinity issues forth a *life spark* of its own essence and passes it into the thought-form. This divine source does so in an attempt to meet humanity halfway, to seek a relationship through which it can communicate with us. The egregore form is thereby given life through this divine emanation and is empowered and animated by it. It has now become a personified conscious god or goddess with the attributes perceived by the worshipers.

The Old Ways tell us that the gods need us as much as we need them. They are maintained by our rituals, providing them nourishment and energy, and by our conscious imagery that sustains their astral connection to us as well as to their own source. This is why gods and goddesses typically belong to a pantheon and have a king and/or queen. What we see in this mythical structure is the acknowledgment of a formula demonstrating that all deities are derived from a higher source (their King and Queen). Again we see the foundation of the occult expression "As above, so below."

The older the egregore, the more powerful it becomes. This is because it takes on an existence of its own and can draw energy from other sources. When a cult disappears, then the egregore either *sleeps* in the mist of the Astral Dimension or accepts another related image through which it can maintain its existence. Examples of this are the ancient goddess forms appearing in images of Virgin Mary manifestations. But if an egregore sleeps instead of transforming, it can be awakened again when worshipers recall its name and perform its rites, as is evidenced in the many reconstructed Traditions of modern Wicca.

It is important to understand that not all gods and goddesses are egregores. The Great God and Goddess have always existed as the Source of All Things prior to the appearance of humankind. These forms are the Archetypes, while the egregores are their children. The Archetypes are the expression of Divine consciousness manifesting in the principles that are the foundation for our Collective Consciousness. Through them we catch a glimpse of the higher nature that formed them.

The Astral Body

Ancient sages taught that the soul, which dwells within our physical body, has a *body of light* called a spirit body (commonly called an astral body today). The soul can leave the physical body by employing this body of light, and does so every evening while the physical body is asleep. Sometimes a soul will only journey out into the Dream Worlds, other times it will travel out into the Astral Worlds. The soul requires nourishment for its body of light, just as the physical body does, and it is through contact with these other realms that the astral body is vitalized and maintained. The teachings tell us that the astral body is connected to the physical body by a "silver cord" of etheric material. As long as it remains intact., this cord will always draw the soul back to the physical body. Once the silver cord is broken, the soul is freed from the physical body, and cannot dwell within it any longer.

The astral body is a duplicate of the physical body that the soul is using in the Physical Dimension. It is this spirit body that we see in dreams, hauntings, and so forth. Some occultists believe that this astral body is what Jesus was using when he reportedly walked on the water, was resurrected, and later appeared to his disciples. Since an astral body does resemble the host body, this is an interesting theory.

The consciousness of the personality (you or me) dwelling within the physical body can be transferred into the astral body, and experience these other realms just as we do this Physical Dimension. It is similar to dreaming, except that we are in control of our own actions and can direct our activities. During the time of the Inquisition, it was extremely dangerous for Witches to gather for their festivals. Therefore, the priestesses and priests of the Old Religion developed an ointment commonly referred to as *Flying Ointment*. It contained many alkaloid ingredients such as belladonna and could "force" an inexperienced Witch out of his or her physical body, thereby causing astral projection of the spirit body to take place. The elders of the coven would then escort the neophytes to the Sabbat in astral form.

Because of the nature of both the hallucinogenic ointment and the Astral Dimension, many wild and preposterous stories were reported by the new Witches concerning what had taken place at the Sabbat. If you've ever been so intoxicated that your friends had to inform you the next day about your actions during the party, then you can relate to what I'm addressing here. The use of drugs among Witches arose from time to time during the Witch trials. The fact that the Inquisitors were not above fabricating a *confession* does not help us sort out the truth of this era in any case. Therefore, it is difficult to gauge the percentage of accusations based on the use of belladonna and other chemicals, as opposed to the imagination of the Inquisitors.

The Hermetic Teachings

The Renaissance produced many manuscripts that collected and chronicled the ancient Occult and Hermetic Arts. Italy, Germany, and England generated some of the most famous and lasting texts that have come down to us today. In fact, many of the English texts are later translations from Latin or Italian. Hermetic philosophy taught that everything created has two bodies, one visible and tangible, and the other invisible and transcendent. The invisible body called the Astrum was part of the material form's nature. The essence of this etheric body was a vital substance called the *archaeus*, which sustained the vitality within all things.

All diseases and maladies of the physical body originated in the astrum. The astrum arose from the energy of the archaeus, which was itself the manifestation of one's rapport with Divinity; in other words, it was the spirituality of the individual. Therefore disease was, in effect, the physical manifestation of imbalance relating to one's invisible spiritual principles. This is very much like the holistic approach that we encounter today in the field of alternative medicine.

Theophrastus of Hohenheim, who took the name of Paracelsus during the Middle Ages, was a great Hermetic philosopher and healer. He was a great supporter of the belief that all illness had its origins in the invisible nature of the physical body, and that illness was the expression of one's spiritual principles. Paracelsus further taught that a person could cause illness within his or her etheric body by his or her own mental attitudes and negative mentality. Healing likewise could be accomplished by the reverse.

The Moon and Astral Energy

In metaphysics the moon is always the instrument of Astral Light. Lunar energy is also presided over by the Moon Goddess. The moon influences the ebb and flow of astral forces just as it influences the tides of our Earth. During its waxing phase from new to full, the moon aids in the formation of astral images. As it wanes from full to new, the moon aids in dissolving poorly formed images. It also serves to dissolve astral forms that are no longer being empowered by thoughts or desires. In the case of forgotten Egregores, the moon can induce a state of *lunar slumber.*

Wicca is a lunar-based magickal system. Its magick has long been focused on the accumulation and direction of the subtle forces of the moon. Even though we speak of Wicca as a magickal system, the art of magick is a personal one despite the basic guidelines. Unlike the ceremonial solar-based magickal systems that demand rigid adherence to ritual structure and procedure, Wiccan magick is intuitive and changes form as does the empowering moon itself.

The Witches of old, from whom modern Wiccans are spiritually descended, were priestesses and priests of the moon. In coastal and island regions they were also known as sea priestesses and priests. The use of sea water was an important aspect in Moon Magick, salt being a crystalline form ideal for absorbing magickal charges. The magickal charging of water and the release of the charge through evaporation is an important aspect. Herbs and pieces of wood from sacred trees were soaked in sea water. Later they were dried and burned as incenses and offerings. The most favored offering was a mixture of cedar, sandalwood, and juniper.

The inner teachings concerning moon magick tell us that the actual essence of the lunar power originates out among the stars. The sun absorbs the stellar radiation and channels it into our solar system. The planets within our solar system absorb this energy, which then merges with their own vibrations or energies. The planets then emanate a composite energy throughout our planetary system. Each planet's energy or vibratory pattern is unique, and influences other planetary forces within each one's sphere of influence. This is the basis of astrology and planetary correspondences in magick; in other words this is how and why it works. The moon absorbs, condenses, and channels all of these forces, which are then channeled to the Earth on the lunar light spectrum. The moon is the focal point of power on the Earth. Without the moon we cannot make use of the universal forces beyond her.

The famous fifteenth-century magician Agrippa spoke of this principle when he wrote:

> ... but the Moon, the nearest to the heavenly influences, by the swiftness of her course, is joined to the sun, and the other planets and stars, as a conception, bringing them forth to the inferior world, as being next to itself, for all the stars have influence on it, being the last receiver, which afterwards communicates the influence of all superiors to these inferiors, and pours them forth upon the Earth... Therefore, her (the moon) motion is to be observed before the others, as the parent of all conception......hence it is, that without the Moon intermediating, we cannot at any time attract the power of the superiors...[1]

Modern science (gradually catching up with ancient knowledge) has now determined that the moon radiates more than reflected light particles. Instruments have now shown that the moon also radiates infrared and microwave frequencies. Infrared emanations are strongest from the first quarter to full, where the levels are four times the amount of radiation compared to the lowest point. It is weakest from the third quarter to the first, being at the lowest emanation at the time of the new moon.

Microwave levels are strongest just after the full moon and new moon, typically reaching their highest levels three days later. In magick the number three is the symbol of manifestation, and in physics microwaves are transmission frequencies. So, in effect, magickal/astral energy under the influence of the moon is carried on the occult counterpart of these lunar emanations. Heat liberates Odic energy, and the infrared

---

1   *Three Books of Occult Philosophy,* 1993.

emanations (heat waves) are highest at the time of the full moon. The full moon is the time when most works of magick are performed, impregnating the Odic mantle of the Earth with thought-forms.

The moon's light is subject to polarization that varies from phase to phase. Polarization in this context is the measurement of light particle density. The most concentrated levels are present when the moon is in its first and third quarters, the latter being its peak level. When the moon is full the polarity is neutral, which increases the electromagnetic field through which the sun, Earth and moon pass (the ecliptical plane). Thus the Odic mantle of the Earth is most stimulated at the time of the full moon.

The Astral Plane

The Astral Plane is not a *place* as we would normally think of when discussing a point in time and space. Neither is it simply a state of consciousness per se. The closest I can come to describing it would be to call it a principle, existing as a condition between the occult worlds. As human beings we possess a body and a brain, yet our spirits and our minds cannot be located in the physical microcosm of our material form.

By way of analogy consider the world of our dreams. We can see objects, experience physical sensations, and feel various emotions. However, we are asleep and our eyes are closed; our physical senses are not being stimulated by external sensations. Our dream world occupies no space. The visual dream images are more than imagination because we experience physical sensations from interactions with them in the dream setting. So we can say that the dream world is not a place or a state of mind. It is a realm with a consciousness of its own, in which our thoughts, fears, and desires become animated in a manner seemingly beyond our control or direction. Dreams are a function of the Astral Plane, but are not the realm itself.

J. H. Brennan points out in his book *Astral Doorways*[2] that we are not transient beings. Our thoughts, memories, and emotions are transient elements of our minds, but we are not any of these things ourselves. They are merely aspects of who and what we are. For example, when we go to a doctor and he or she asks us how we are, we often reply the we are in pain because of an injury to some part of our body. The truth is actually that we are not in pain but rather that some part of our body is in pain. There is a difference between saying "my hand is in pain" and saying "I'm in pain because my hand was slammed in the car door." The former is an understanding that our bodies are simply vehicles that carry our souls around. The latter is a claim that we are the physical bodies that our souls inhabit. This is an important magickal distinction.

It is important to the understanding of the Astral Plane and its workings to understand something of what we call the Self. We are, in effect, a divine spark of consciousness extended (and some say separated) from the Source-of-All-Things. This consciousness some people call the spirit or the soul. We exist within physical bodies in the material world. When we consider the Self we can picture it at the center of a microcosmic universe. Our immediate surroundings have the greatest influence upon us, and we upon them. Unless we hold some important office or position of great influence we typically only indirectly impact the community in which we live.

From there the world slips into shades of lesser influence. For example, our votes individually have less impact in a state election than in a city election, and so forth. As a citizen of a country we have even less impact on other countries, yet we are still connected in increasingly diluted ways. However, the actions of countries and higher forms of government affect us greatly on an individual basis. This is also true of the planes of existence themselves. On an astral level, the same is true of our consciousness. We begin with an awareness of our indi-

---

2   Brennan, J. H. *Astral Doorways* (New York: Samuel Weiser Inc., 1971), pp. 1–10.

viduality and its wants and needs. Then we acknowledge the immediate environment in which we dwell and how it impacts us. Next we acknowledge the influence of other embodied souls whom we encounter. From there we move to our subconscious awareness, followed by the influence of the Collective Consciousness of our race, a symbolic return to the greater aspect of which we are but a spark.

In the vast majority of cases the soul or spirit of an individual enters into the physical dimension from the Astral because of its need to learn and experience various things. The soul possesses a rudimentary awareness of what it must accomplish and how to go about it. This is not unlike the inherent knowledge within newborn animals that allows them to survive until they can defend and care for themselves. Later this same inner knowledge will allow them to build nests or burrows appropriate to their own species. In this respect the soul possesses the basic survival skills that manifest in what we call the intuition. Through this we can discern many experiences that we will encounter in any given lifetime. The danger here lies in allowing ourselves to be both teacher and student at the same time. Though we can learn many things by ourselves we cannot teach ourselves what we do not already know. To understand the real difference between learning and teaching is one of the keys to personal enlightenment.

Just as the Self can be divided into levels of lower, middle, and higher, so can the Astral realm be divided. In most cases we generally speak of the Higher and Lower Astral Levels because they impact us the most. In effect the Astral Plane is a meeting place where divine consciousness and human consciousness have interaction (the Higher and the Lower levels). Both forms of consciousness impregnate the Astral Light and are the root causes of manifestation. There are seven planes: Physical, Elemental, Astral, Mental, Spiritual, Divine, and Ultimate. Stimulating one plane causes a ripple which brings all planes into reaction. This is the basic formula that allows both prayers and magickal acts to be effective tools.

The Middle level of the Astral Plane is the realm in which egregores have their influence and function. Because egregores are composite beings derived partly from the energy of human consciousness and partly from divine (see page 92), it is here in the Middle level of the Astral Plane that magick can pass or fail. It is here that the *Lords of Karma* take note of what transpires on the lower worlds. Secret societies create signs, symbols, and gestures that allow individuals to gain access to the deeper levels of the Astral Plane. Beings known as Watchers oversee these societies and can aid or obstruct the magickal workings of any occult society. The symbolism displayed by witches, for example, announces their beliefs and creeds. If a Wiccan violates his or her own tenets, then it draws a response from the Watchers.

Divination and the Astral Plane

As noted in this chapter, the thoughts and deeds occurring in the physical world are imprinted on the Odic mantle of the Earth. The resulting energy patterns then influence the Pranic field, and due to the electromagnetic nature of Odic material these patterns adhere to the pranic level that we call the Akashic Records. The Collective Consciousness of our race is vitalized and maintained by the energies contained in this akashic energy field. Our subconscious minds are linked to the Collective Consciousness through the Dream World that opens up into it. As I stated earlier, dreams are a function of the Astral Plane, and therefore these energy patterns merge with the astral material.

The astral images that form as a result of our in-flowing thoughts, deeds, and desires cause responding forms to arise in the Astral Light. Divination is the ability to discern these patterns and their logical outcome. Whether we use Tarot cards, runes, palmistry, or other divinatory tools, we are simply focusing the mind so that it can read the astral patterns. Ancient symbolism appearing in Tarot cards and runes serves as a symbol of the Collective Consciousness. In effect they are the keys and passwords that allow us access into the Astral Light. The Watchers on the planes observe and understand the signs we display in these divinatory tools and they aid us in our quest.

It is important to understand that divination only reveals the patterns that are forming in one's future. Nothing is fixed and absolute. When we divine something we are actually saying that if nothing alters the forming patterns, then such and such lies in store. When we access the Higher Astral level we can see what might be called the Divine Patterns or Stellar Patterns. These are the major events of one's life that the gods set in place. We see them reflected in astrology, in the natal chart. However, even these patterns can be altered by a variety of things. Every human possesses the gift of free will. With this gift comes a great responsibility because not only can we alter the course of our own lives with the choices we make, we can alter the course of other people's lives.

The myth of Odin and the runes is perhaps one of the best teachings concerning the power of divination. In the myth, Odin sacrifices himself and hangs from a branch on the World Tree for nine nights. His side has been pierced with a spear, and his blood drips down on the ground beneath him. Later, nearing death, he notices the appearance of magickal runes below him. With great effort he reaches out to them and once he has them in his hands he is freed from the World Tree and is vitalized with the essence of magickal power from the runes.

It is no coincidence to find this symbolism expressed in the Tarot card of the Hanged Man. The Hanged Man symbolizes the condition of the human soul, metaphysically suspended by a cord from the higher planes. What appears as fatality ends up becoming enlightenment. This is the key to understanding divination and the future. Fate does not rule, and fatality is not the end result. The Fortune Teller hangs suspended over the World of Illusion and perceives the magickal symbolism of the patterns. He or she is not focused on the fatalistic drops of blood but rather on their transformation into self-empowering keys. The purpose of divination is to inform us of the patterns woven into the fabric of our lives so that we can allow them to form or take actions to alter their formation. It is not the purpose of divination to prepare us for the inevitable.

———————

Chapter Seven

The Odic Force

*The spiral energy associated with the
serpent force is symbolic of movement.
Movement is key to the understanding
of the Odic Force.*

In the famous movie *Star Wars* we were introduced to a mystical concept known as the *Force,* and a sect of spiritual warriors known as *Jedi* Knights. Ancient Sages have long taught the existence of a Universal Power that is the very fabric of magick. Eliphas Levi, an occultist whose writings inspired such famous figures as Aleister Crowley, A. E. Waite, MacGregor Mathers, and Dion Fortune, wrote extensively of this in his works on the Astral Light. An integral aspect of this Light was the force known as Od. Franz Mesmer, who helped establish hypnotism as a science, was known to have studied the ancient Hermetic books of the Renaissance and he showed a particular interest in the writings of Paracelsus. From his studies he developed the theory of animal magnetism and the presence of magnetic fluids in the human body.

Levi spoke of the Odic Force as being a substance as indifferent to *movement* as it is to *rest.* He taught that nothing was truly at rest or in movement because one evoked the other and always resulted in an eventual state of equilibrium. Levi said that a *fixed* nature attracts a *volatile* nature in order to *fix* it, and that volatile attracts fixed in order to *volatize* it. He often referred to the principle underlying this force as *Elementary Matter.* Essentially, one thing can only be defined by the existence of its opposite. In other words, to understand what *negative* is, one must understand what *positive* is.

Levi taught that the Odic Force, although not identifiable with the forces of electricity and magnetism, is essentially the basis for the laws of physics as applied to such forces. The Odic Force is present everywhere in time and space. In quantum mechanics we might say that something is everywhere at once, but at the same time can be more discernable at a specific point. So too is the nature of Od, and we can say that the Odic Force is more concentrated in one thing than in another. Therefore we find the presence of this force most noted in stellar radiation, electromagnetic fields, chemical reactions, metabolic function, and crystal formations. All of these aspects can be found in the ancient arts of Alchemy and Witchcraft.

Elemental Energy

I have separated this topic from that discussed in the chapter on the Elements so as to avoid confusion. In this section I am not speaking of Elemental energy relating to the individual forces of Earth, Air, Fire, and Water. I am speaking instead of that force which underlies it all. Electrical and magnetic energies arise from the nature of the Four Elements. Magnetic energy is derived from the Water Element and electrical energy comes from the Fire Element. Therefore we can say that such things as Odic, Prana, Mana, and Occult Magnetism are all parts of Elementary energy.

Prana is an occult term for the Life Principle or the *breath of life* in all living things. Mana is the indwelling force of *vitality* existing in all material objects. Some people may argue that Mana exists in all life-forms as well, because they are also material objects. Mana is raw, unconscious energy that exists within physical material and automatically shapes itself around concepts, condensing and empowering them. In a sense, one can say that it is the Microcosm to the Macrocosm of Astral Light, except that it is not *conscious* in the same way as is Astral Light. When we feel the power or energy of a place (such as Stonehenge or the Great Pyramid), what we are sensing is the accumulation of its Mana. Occult magnetism is an agent that emanates the phenomena of attraction, repulsion, and polarity.

The etheric property of Elemental energy is the vehicle through which material forms manifest. We may refer to it as pre-matter in order to think of it in simpler terms. To illustrate the mechanics of this we can liken it to the emanations of Prana in Eastern Mysticism. Cosmic matter known as Prakriti emanates out from the Divine Source and is channeled to the sun. The sun in turn channels this vital energy into the bound ether of the Earth's atmosphere, where it merges with the chemicals contained in the air we breathe. Thus the atmosphere itself becomes a source of energy to the spiritual faculties of souls dwelling within material bodies. The soul or spirit is fed by the pranic charges breathed in through the lungs.

The thoughts, words, and deeds of our race are imprinted on the Prana, forming what is known as the *Akashic Records* (see glossary). The vibration of the Earth's Prana extends to the bound Pranic field of the sun through gravitational forces, and thus *communicates* back to the cosmic emanation of Prana itself (The Source of All Things). This is what many people refer to as the domino chain, where tipping one domino in a

standing row creates a chain reaction, tripping the rest. Therefore what we plant in the *bound ether* of the Earth, we also
plant in the "pre-matter," which in turn stimulates the higher
or Spiritual levels of existence. The higher planes then respond
to the influx of energy and we become subject to the down-
pour of Astral Light from above. It is in this Light that
prophets and other Holy Ones speak to us of Divine messages.

Human emotions are a powerful force. From them we have
been driven to topple empires, create great literature, express
and deeply experience love, and to create beautiful temples to
our gods and goddesses. In a magickal sense emotion equates
with magnetism. If the emotions rise, so does the emanation
of magnetic energy. Elemental energy flows into the human
aura and empowers the mind of the individual. In this respect
he or she can tap into the surrounding Odic Force, impregnating it with images raised and carried on the emotions.
Sound acts to liberate the Odic Force. This is the basis for
chanting, and for musical instruments employed in ritual settings. Rhythmic physical movement will also free Odic energies, thus we have the foundation for ritual dance. Lastly, Fire
will release condensed fields of Odic energy and so we see the
ancient employment of bonfires for Pagan gatherings.

The Odic Force

In ancient times the Odic Force was symbolized by the serpent
and specifically by the Great Python. This was the symbolism
employed at the ancient oracle of Delphi, whose original name
was Pytho. According to legend, a great serpent inhabited the
chasms within the oracle cave. The god Apollo slew the creature
and cast it down into the pit over which the oracle seat was suspended. A priestess sat on this seat. Legend has it that the fumes
from the decaying serpent rose up and imparted to her the
power of prophecy. In a metaphysical sense we can say that
heat (Apollo being the sun god) released the power of the accumulated Odic force (the serpent) that allowed the priestess to

discern the patterns forming within the astral plane (prophecy). chapter six contains connective information and you may want to review it for a more involved study.

The Occult Serpent as a force is divided into the twin serpents of the magickal staff of Hermes. Here we find two serpents, one white and one black, entwined around a staff upon which sits a winged sphere. The staff as a whole depicts the equilibrium of contrary forces culminating in harmony. Od, as the white serpent, represents the active power of magnetism directed by the personal will of the Magus—in other words, the power to make our own choices, our free will. Ob, as the black serpent, represents the passive power of magnetism directed by patterns already established in the Astral Plane. This can be said to be Fate or Destiny playing a role in one's life. The winged sphere represents the point between Fate and personal will, which we call Aour. Levi tells us that the secret of employing the Odic Force lies in this: "To rule the fatality of the Ob *by intelligence and the power of the Od* so as to create the perfect balance of Aour."

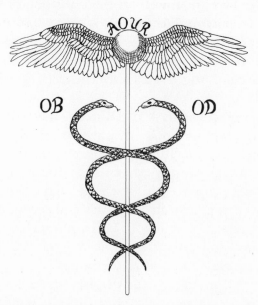

The Magical Staff of Hermes, uniting Od and Ob.

The Astral Light, also known as the Great Magickal Agent, can be controlled by two things: first by fixing the mind on the image of the desire, and second by projecting energy into the astral material. This is accomplished by generating the Odic Force through emotional investment. Such a disturbance of the ether engages the electromagnetic properties of the Odic Force, which in turn stirs the Astral Light. Within the malleable substance of the Astral Light, the projected images form into active vessels by personal will and imagination. By moving with the flow of this occult formula, one's magick is not deflected. The moving charge of the emotions (electrical) passes along the magnetic field of the Odic Mantle, and thus gains access into the astral level. Carried within this current is the image focused by the mind, around which the Astral Light will then form.

Manifestation occurs when division takes place between the Od and Ob. Manifestation dissolves when the division is resolved by equilibrium or is absorbed back into Aour by unity initiated from a higher power (the so-called *will of the gods*). This holds true as well for the transition of forms from one plane to another. For manifestation to continue down to the next lower plane the polarities of its Od and Ob natures must exist in their extreme opposite natures without equilibrium. Once equilibrium takes place, the form manifests on that specific plane.

To accomplish this task the Wiccan must conjure up the image of the opposite poles of one's desire, while not losing sight of their equilibrium. You must sustain the desire as an image while maintaining awareness of the polarities. If one wishes to bring about a manifestation from a lower to a higher plane, one conceives its opposites and reconciles the pair through imagination and will. This again is the opposite, and so we sustain the polarities while maintaining the desired image. The easiest method of accomplishing this seemingly difficult task is to employ the magickal caduceus image. The desired goal is sigilized and placed in the winged orb. The polarities of the desired goal are sigilized and placed next to the heads of the serpents. The positive polarity is set next to the Od serpent and the negative polarity is set next to the Ob serpent. By focusing the mind on the sigils one can raise magickal energy to empower the spell without having to consciously hold the image of the desire and its polarities in one's thoughts.

When we divide any pair of related aspects in order to bring about a manifestation, we actually end up increasing their attraction to one another. This is because we disturb their energy fields and cause them to unequally exchange their magnetism. Due to a loss of the magnetism that originally held them in equilibrium, a repulsion occurs. Once the new level of magnetism stabilizes, it creates a recharged magnetic field in each of the separated components. This in turn creates an attraction of their fields to one another and the more magnetic of the two will *bleed off* magnetic energy to the lesser. The electromagnetic charge passes back and forth as an alternating current, wherein their relative potency is not fixed but is instead dependent on the vitality of energy involved.

This formula is essential to consistently successful works of magick. The following will serve to illustrate a practical application of the magickal caduceus technique. To bring good luck into my life, I use the chart in appendix two called the "Magickal Values of the Moon," to sigilize the polarities of luck. I sigilize the word "misfortune" and draw the symbol next to the head of the Ob serpent. Then I sigilize the word "windfall" and place it next to the head of the Od serpent. In the orb of Aour, I place the sigil of the word "luck." To conclude the work of magick I raise odic energy by stimulating the emotions. Keeping my eyes focused on the three sigils, I exhale odic breath upon the caduceus. When I have released all my energy, I fold the Od and Ob serpents back so that only the Aour sigil shows. My final act is to put the caduceus in a metal bowl with some incense and ignite it. The heat will disperse the odic energy into the incense smoke. Be outside, or near an open window, so that the energy passes directly into the atmosphere. Don't worry if you do not fully comprehend the formula at this point, because it is the purpose of this book to provide the concepts and tools by which this understanding is made accessible.

The key lies in the understanding of basic magickal principles, along with an understanding of the serpent forces of Od and Ob. However, another mystery of magick lies in the fact that some people already know the formula intuitively, but may never have put it into words or concepts. They use it all the time and never know it as a formula. On a mundane level if we pass an electrical beam through the open ends of a horseshoe magnet the beam will be deflected. However, if we pass it in a parallel manner across the magnetic poles then no deflection takes place. In a magickal sense it was for this reason that the ancients mapped out the appropriate times for employing such things as lunar phases and planetary hours. While there is a lot to be said for intuitive magick, we must still work within the laws of Nature and the Supernatural in order to ensure continuity of success. Otherwise there can be a tendency for our magick to be "hit or miss." In other words, you can do the right thing at the right time by coincidence or dumb luck—but I am not dismissing the value of intuition. Wicca is a lunar consciousness and therefore it can weave its way in and out of the magickal linear structures of solar consciousness. Yet it must be remembered that, above all, Wicca is a Nature religion and is subject to the metaphysical laws reflected in the ways of Nature itself.

Principles of Od and Ob

In the ancient Mystery Traditions of pre-Christian Europe, Occultists spoke of the Universal Agent. During the Middle Ages this was known as the Great Magical Arcanum. It was represented in all Mystery Sects by the serpent figure. In Western Occultism this agent was depicted as twin serpents, each symbolizing a certain aspect of the Force itself. In its active nature it was called Od and in its passive nature it was called Ob. When the two Forces were said to be in equilibrium, the resulting state was called Aour.

Eliphas Levi described Od as magnetism controlled by the will of the operator. He referred to Ob as a passive clair-voyance called Trance. The synthesis of the life-giving Od and the death-giving Ob he called the Aour. Passive Astral Light is symbolized by the mythological spirit of the Python. The Scepter of Hermes or Rod of Aesculapius rec-onciles the serpents of Od and Ob. Harmony arises from the analogy of contraries.

The occult concept of Duality is reflected in the caduceus figure. Ancient symbols retained this teaching and secret prac-tices were established on this principle. The Tarot card of the Magician depicting one hand raised upward and the other pointing down is a good example. The black and white pillars marking entrances to ancient Mystery Temples are another such example. Employing the number three, symbolic of man-ifestation, in rituals and works of magick expresses the duality held in equilibrium. This is the Od and Ob resulting in Aour. This is the Great Astral Triad.

In *Transcendental Magic*, first published in 1896, Levi says:

> *Equilibrium is the consequence of two forces. If two forces are absolutely and invariably equal, the equilibrium will be immobility and therefore the negation of life. Movement is the result of an alternative preponderance. The impulsion given to one of the sides of a balance necessarily determines the motion of the other. Thus contraries act on one another, throughout all Nature, by correspondence and analogical connection.*[1]

Levi is speaking of the bleeding off and the alternating cur-rent to which I referred earlier concerning magickal formula.

---

1   Levi, Eliphas. Transcendental Magic. (New York: Samuel Weiser, 1974), p. 213.

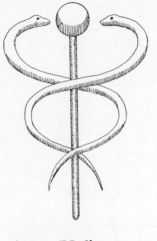

Aegean/Mediterranean Caduceus.

The flow of this current is represented by the movement of the serpents around the magickal caduceus (see illustration). Two types of current are symbolized in the magickal caduceus image, one a spiral (the serpents) and the other a linear emanation (the shaft). The rod of the caduceus is divided into vertically shaded halves, one white and the other black. The current of Ob is the serpent of fate and arises from the black half. The current of Od is the serpent of free will that arises from the white side. Seated on the rod is the orb of the moon, symbolic of the energy of equilibrium that oversees the serpent forces and keeps them in harmony.

The spiral energy associated with the serpent force is symbolic of movement. Movement is key to the understanding of the Odic Force. Astral Light forms around the energy of concentrated thoughts. Thought-forms disturb the astral material creating stress lines and flow lines within its etheric substance. The Od and Ob currents then become divided. Thus the equilibrium is offset and must be restored by the nature of the Universe itself. Therefore it must be made manifest in order to bring its polarities back into harmony. This act of division initiates the forces which will then create a new form. As was noted earlier in this chapter, once equilibrium takes place the form will manifest.

Kenneth Grant in his book *Cults of the Shadow* [2] associates the forces of Ob and Od to Chokmah and Binah of the Kabbalistic Tradition. He connects them with African Magick and assigns these forces to Obatala and Odudua, the chief god and goddess of the primal African pantheon. Grant also

2 Grant, Kenneth. *Cults of the Shadow* (New York: Samuel Weiser, 1976), pp. 23–27.

reveals the correspondence between Od and Od and the Ida and Pingala currents employed in the Tantric Tradition. These are, of course, the left and right branches of the ganglionic nerve structure symbolizing the lunar and solar power currents within the human body (see illustration, right). In the Tantric Tradition the sleeping force of Ultimate Personal Power resides at the base of the spine and is called the *Kundalini* or Serpent Power.

In ancient Egypt the headdress of the pharaoh featured a serpent on the forehead. The ancient Pharaohs were believed to be descended from the gods and therefore actual divine beings themselves. To raise the Ida and Pingala serpent forces upward into the brow chakra (third eye) is one of the goals of Tantric magick. With the serpent consciousness dwelling in the brow chakra, great psychic powers become readily available to the individual. Thus the serpent headdress represented the equilibrium of the serpent forces held in consciousness by the divine ruler of Egypt.

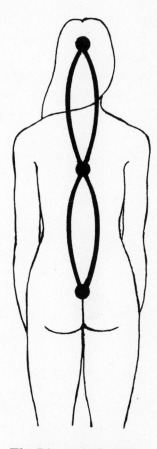

The Ida and Pingala Currents.

The Solar and Lunar currents of electrical and magnetic energy as reflected in the left and right branches of the ganglionic nerve structure.

What we may be seeing here are the Mediterranean roots of ancient African religions that are themselves the origins of such religions as Santeria and Macumba. There are many similarities between Santeria and Stregheria, for example, specifically in the association of saints with ancient gods and goddesses. Both religions also incorporate a deep respect and honoring of one's ancestors. It does seem that once we strip away the cultural aspects of ethnicity within Pagan systems we come face to face with many universal magickal concepts. Truth is truth, no matter who speaks it.

Chapter Eight

The Art of Magick

We can generally say that magick is a matter of vibrational cause and effect. Essentially, we disturb the bound etheric atmosphere of our planet and certain things result.

To *know,* to *will,* to *dare,* to be *silent;* these are the words of the Magickal Master. To know something we must do more than satisfy our curiosity, we must study not only the concept but those things that relate to the concept. To will we must endure without yielding to defeat or discouragement; we must know our path and walk it despite its obstacles. To dare we must be willing to accept the risks of disfavor and mistreatment; we must be true to the path we walk whether the road is smooth, or covered with pitfalls and jagged rocks. To be silent we must simply speak our truths without pretension or vanity.

One of the major attractions to Wicca for the beginner is often the practice of magick. Just as there are many misconceptions about Wicca, there are also many concerning the art of magick, or even magick itself. True magick is the ability to bring about the manifestation of personal (or group) desire. This is accomplished by one's ability to collect, focus, and direct enough "raw" energy with which to create the desired manifestation. All magickal operations begin within the mind and are directed outward. The subconscious mind works through corresponding images under the direction of the conscious mind. There are many different ways of employing magick and many different aspects of magick. Basically speaking, however, most types of magick will fall into one of two methods, and these are called "raised" or "drawn."

Raised energy emanates from the body and/or mental sphere of the person. Drawn energy is attracted in from other realms, usually by ritual methods. This includes workings that involve gods and/or spirits. Magick may also fall into the realms of "black magick," which is negative, and "white magick," which is positive. There is also a third type referred to as "gray magick" that is a blend of the two. Wiccans understand the laws of Nature and of Karma, and therefore do not practice black magick. It is an old teaching that the type of energy we send out will come back to us "threefold." There is a need for clear thinking when it comes to employing a work of magick.

Many people think that magick has no basis in scientific fact. This is not correct; the laws of physics provide many reasons why magick does indeed *work*. These reasons are based on energy fields and various currents existing around the Earth. Energy currents are caused by the rotation of the Earth and the gravitational forces of the sun and the moon, as well as other celestial bodies. The actual spinning of the Earth creates electromagnetic currents within our *bound* atmosphere. As the Earth moves around the Sun, stress is created on the Earth by the sun's gravity. This stress causes vibrational currents in our atmosphere as well.

Positive currents of stress flow from east to west across our planet. There are also seasonal tides that are based on fluctuations of the electromagnetic current surrounding the Earth, corresponding to the position of the sun and the Earth. Positive (electrical) tides flow from late March to late September. Negative (magnetic) tides flow from late September to late March. The religious festivals of Wicca mark the peak times of each of these currents.

We can generally say that magick is a matter of vibrational *cause* and *effect.* Essentially, we *disturb* the bound etheric atmosphere of our planet and certain things result. It is the art of magick to *impregnate* the ether with our formed desires and then to direct them to manifest. The major difference is whether the ripple is sent out or brought down. Magick that deals with the invocations of spirits and/or deities incorporates the vibrations theory as a catalyst. The forces behind magick are real, being both natural and supernatural. It is the art of getting these forces to work for you, and not against you, that is the Art of Magick.

Ritual magick works on the basis of attracting sympathetic energies by means of words (which are vibrations), gestures, and dramatic portrayals. The theory here is that the combination of these factors directed by the person or group *will,* and boosted by the need/desire, will attract sympathetic energies. These energies will then cause a *ripple* in the necessary plane resulting in manifestation. Everything that is now a physically created object was once only a concept.

The book you are reading these words in was once merely an idea in my mind. Various people working for the publisher had to mentally *form the image* that was to become this book. Once visualized they could then proceed to take the steps necessary to cause their *thought-forms* to become a physical book. This is essentially the formula for magick. The tools and articles used in a ritual setting serve to trigger or stimulate the participants so that the necessary energies can be raised. The tools which are used in a ritual also act as extensions of the ritualist's *will power* and mental/psychic abilities.

Everything placed into a magickal operation serves to gradually induce a change in consciousness within the person or persons involved in its performance. Candles, robes, chanting, and the actual setting up of the altar and casting of the circle all contribute to this evolution of Consciousness from mundane to magickal. This is also one of the reasons why many Wiccans choose Craft names, such as "Ladyhawke," for example. This allows a person to become something beyond who and what they are in the mundane world. Plain ol' Suzie may not be able to perform magick, but once within the ritual circle Ladyhawke certainly can.

Magnetism

When we speak of magnetic energies or forces in an occult context, we are speaking of the metaphysical counterpart of the physical plane expression. Among initiates the magnetic force is an extremely refined substance that can be controlled and directed by the mind. It can be condensed and *stored* in inanimate objects. These objects then become *charged* objects. Experience has shown that liquids of any kind, and all metals, will readily accept and store an occult magnetic charge. Wood or wood products will accept a charge, but will not store it for long periods of time. Silk is the only known fabric to date that will not accept or store this type of charge. For this reason it is used as insulation against occult magnetic charges and magnetic contamination. Thus it is useful to wrap charged objects in silk so that the magnetic charge does not leak away from the charged object.

The power to employ occult magnetism can also be termed *fascination* or *enchantment*. Basically there are two methods of using personal magnetism. One is to impregnate the aura of another person with a thought-form generated by your own mind. The other is to persuade the individual so that their own personal will shapes the thought-form. This may be accomplished by accumulating energy within your own aura for projection, by physically touching the other person, by projecting the magickal vapor through the eyes, or by the tonal quality of your voice.

The vibrational qualities of the voice carry personal magnetism, stimulating the etheric substance of astral light. There is a direct link to the spoken word and to the breath. From an occult perspective, the element of air is the mediating element between electrical and magnetic energy. Through slow deep breathing and emotional arousal the blood accumulates odic energy from the pranic atmosphere around us. This charged blood passes through the lungs, imparting magnetic energy into the breath. When merged with the personal desire of the individual, a powerful thought-form can be created within this magnetic field. It can be projected out through the eyes by focusing upon a person or an object, holding in the breath, and visualizing a stream of vapor passing out through the eyes as though you were exhaling through them. The key to employing elemental energy is strongly linked to controlled breathing because the breath can be strongly charged with odic energy.

Warming the breath (from a deep inhale) carries an electrical charge and cool breath (blown from a shallow puff of air) carries a magnetic charge. This is apparent when the breath is applied to another person just at the base of their cerebellum. A puff will send a magnetic current into the person's aura, resulting in an electrical response. Usually this is annoying to the person and you get a startled reaction, an electrical snap. A slow exhale from deep within the lungs sends an electrical current resulting in a magnetic response. This is usually an erotic response, the receptive magnetic energy associated with sexual submission.

When employing odic breath in connection with any life-form, an opposite polarity will result: magnetic breath evokes an electrical response and an electrical breath evokes a magnetic response. When using breath charges on inanimate objects, the active charge is delivered without a polarity response. An exception to this rule is any inanimate object already bearing a magickal charge, or any magnetized object. Essentially you will want to bear in mind that magnetic energies draw, and electrical energies vitalize. With experimentation you will also find that magnetic energies can sometimes deflect directed charges, just as electrical energies can sometimes cause inertia.

For healing purposes you will generally want to use a magnetic breath so that the electrical response will accelerate the healing process. This is particularly effective with wounds, burns, and other short-term injuries. An electrical breath is best used in the healing of long-term illnesses only when using other magickal techniques in conjunction. The magnetic response is useful in allowing the illness to be receptive to other types of magickal energy directed toward the patient. Electrical breath will also enhance the effects of medication.

Magickal Energy

When you hold your hands a few inches apart, palms facing, you create an electromagnetic field between them. This magnetism indicates the presence of polarities: opposite poles that attract one another. The first thing we can say about magickal energy is that it is composed of opposites. The best way to understand these opposites is to think of them as directions of force:

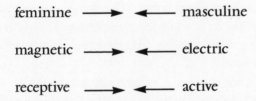

feminine ⟶ ⟵ masculine

magnetic ⟶ ⟵ electric

receptive ⟶ ⟵ active

Although we divide them to talk about them, these opposites within energy can never be separated. One cannot exist without the other. Positive and negative pulls are both necessary for movement. Together the two create vibration. When opposites are in the correct relationship the result is balance. When they are not in balance then they are negative and destructive.

The second thing we can say about energy is that it is balanced. Balance is the natural state of the Universe. However, when energy becomes plural it is reduced to positive and negative charges and is considered unbalanced. Because they are incomplete forms of the *Universal All,* these energies create a separation between the whole and its parts. These separations manifest physically and mentally. Held as such they must occupy definable territories. You may have noticed this in yourself, perhaps as a sadness in the heart area or fear in the pit of your stomach; these are energies occupying space.

When energies are held in by emotion they can be felt as a weight or a presence. Ego can bind energy within us. Ego separates us from the All. The truth is that we are no more or less than anything around us. Everything is a physical manifestation of energy in its state of positive and negative charges. The effects of magick are worked through the aspect of energy— sometimes called *od* or *odic* force. It is the vital element which flows through all terrestrial globes and all living beings. By its various influences, this agent attracts some things to others, and keeps other things away as well. The human body radiates this energy and can influence and affect people and situations in the general vicinity.

The Odic force is capable of being consciously developed, energized, and intensified. It is this power, concentrated and directed, that is the basis of personal magick. The will of the person performing a work of such magick concentrates and controls the energy. This concentration of energy is then sent to its goal, either stored in a talisman or sent in a thought-form to the person or thing to be affected. The power of the Odic force must be used in accordance with the solar and lunar tides, as well as the Cosmic Tides.

When I speak of energy polarity, I am speaking of magickal energy. It is an old teaching that each of us has within
ourselves an energy current composed of masculine and feminine polarities (active and receptive). When we raise magick,
or draw magick, we cannot help but give it dual polarity,
because that is our own inner nature. In the Eastern mystical
traditions they would call this the *Ida* and *Pingala* currents.
These currents originate at the base of the spine, divide and
flow up from the base chakra, cross at the heart chakra and
then flow into the third eye uniting once again (see illustration, chapter seven, page 117).

If we take the old Occult axiom "As above, so below" we can
also say that the Creators set within all things this same Ida
and Pingala nature (since it would be the divine imprint within anything created). The nature of the artist is always within
the nature of his or her art, so what I am speaking of is the
etheric essence of energy. The occult nature of a physical
object, or a principle of physics, is not always readily apparent.
That is why it is called "Occult," which means "hidden" or
"secret."

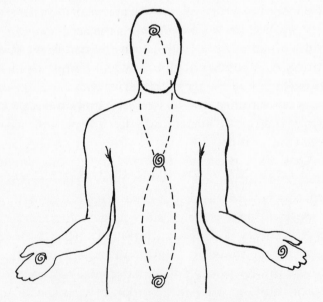

Electrical and Magnetic Currents.

All the actions of magickal manifestation take place within the Astral Dimension. From a magickal perspective, time and space do not exist as commonly understood by the scientific community. Magick has unlimited range per se, because it does not travel in a linear manner. Instead it permeates the astral sphere of our world and behaves (from our perspective) as though it had infinite range because it manifests without reference to distance. One way to think of this is to think of blowing a puff of air into a balloon. The breath inside the balloon is everywhere, touching on the interior walls of the balloon. You can access the breath on any point along the surface of the sphere of the balloon because it is already present there.

Essentially we can say that magick travels at the speed of thought, whatever that might be. Magickal energy is affected by a variety of external forces. Magickal force fields, such as protective pentacles, can slow or deflect the force. This is not unlike the flow of an electron beam being diverted when it crosses perpendicular to a magnetic field. Greater forces such as those exerted by deity or high-level spirits can also alter the course of one's magick. Basically there are only two reasons why one's magick will ever fail: it was performed incorrectly or inappropriately, or a greater force opposes or diverts it. In the final analysis, magick is based on the consistent and reliable laws of metaphysics. I suspect we may someday discover that magick and quantum mechanics are intimately related. In any case if you know, understand, and apply the appropriate formula, then your magick will not fail you.

The Craft and Magickal Energy

There are many different types and styles of magick involved in the practice of Wiccan magick. Some covens/practitioners differ in the type used; some use all and some may combine only a few techniques. Basically magick may be organized into two categories: operative and ceremonial. The first covers spells, words of power, the use of unguents/potions, etc. The second is concerned with the operation of Craft rituals. The aspects of magick can be thought of in this manner: sympathetic, ritual, raised, drawn, and sex magick.

Ritual is a means of concentrating and attracting those energies that are symbolized through the use of gestures, word phrases and images (symbols, runes, etc). The magickal theory being that by acting out certain symbolic gestures, with concentration on their meanings, one can attract sympathetic energies inherent throughout the Universe. These energies can be directed by the use of one's controlled will. This aspect is sometimes called the Witches' pyramid.

The Witches' pyramid is a glyph which symbolizes the mentality necessary for the directed manifestation of magickal energy. It is composed of these attributes: personal will, imagination, and visualization. All three of these must enclose the expectation of success.

Will

•

(Expectation)

•   •

Imagination   Visualization

Expectation is essential to a successful manifestation. You must *will* a thing to be, imagine the outcome in your mind, and visualize what it is that you desire. Beyond this you must have the expectation that it will manifest as you desire it to. The Elemental Plane (also known as the Plane of Forces) flows like a river to and from the Physical dimension and the Astral Dimension. It is this plane which carries magickal energy to the Astral Plane where it takes on the image of the desired effect. Once the thought is formed there, it then passes back through the Elemental Plane and manifests upon the Physical.

Sex magick is the use of energy raised through sexual union. This is the most condensed and powerful form of energy that can be raised from the human body. Some Craft Traditions employ it in the Third Degree Initiation ceremony. In Eastern mystical traditions it is known as Tantra. The ancient Egyptians employed it as well. The energy raised in sex magick is sometimes referred as the *Kundalini* power, or serpent power. The serpent headdress of ancient Egyptian rulers (see page 117) is symbolic of the serpent power having been raised to the third eye, the sign of Divine Union, or *Samadhi*. The Kundalini force is seated at the base of the spine and governs the sexual nature of the individual. In magick it is drawn up through each of the chakra points to the third eye, employing sexual energy as the energy of propulsion.

The Imagination and Will

Among those who do not practice magick, it is quite common to find an attitude that *imagination* is purely fantasy. To a practitioner of magick, however, imagination is a vapor that can carry thought-forms into the astral levels through the subconscious doorway. On the Physical Plane a person's thoughts in imagination can manifest as a novel, a movie, or a work of art. On the Astral Plane a person's imagination can manifest as an etheric image. This image can be as real to astral entities as any physical form is to material beings.

Consistently effective magick requires the actions of both the imagination and the personal will. The will by itself is an undefined current of energy. The imagination by itself lacks vitality. When the two factors are brought together, substantial magickal effects are possible. In practical application the Wiccan must first evoke the imagination so that an image of the desired effect is created. Then the personal will must be used to direct the energy of the imagination.

Eastern Mystics call the creative power of the imagination *Kriya Sakti*. They view the imagination as the womb, and the will as the impregnating seed. When joined together they can produce the magickal child of external manifestation. It must be understood that *will* is not the same thing as *desire.* The personal will is an act of concentration and must be kept separate from desire. The imagination arises from desire and is vitalized by the will. Therefore the mind must be free of desire when focusing the will upon the image evoked by the imagination. This is why symbols and sigils are favored by the magician because they address the goal of manifestation and not the desired effect itself.

Magickal Links

All things connected with a person contain an energy link with that person. For example, a person's hair holds the vibrations of his or her energy pattern, and by the use of sympathetic magick that person can be influenced by energy directed to him or her. This could be used for emotional healing of that person, motivation, or whatever. The hair acts as a point of concentration and as a kind of "homing device" for the directed energy. The same is true for unwashed items of clothing and other personal items. By making an image of an individual and placing his/her personal items within it, one creates a center of focus.

Works of magick for the gain of something should be done while the moon is waxing (new to full) and works to be rid of something or to undo something should be performed when the moon is waning. The full moon is the time of peak power when the forces of Light and Darkness are in total balance. Essentially any and all works of magick are possible at this time, and portals to the Astral Plane are most open to access during this lunar phase.

Cord magick is a basic magickal technique in Witchcraft. The theory is that by concentrating a desire on the cords, using them as a focus, one can raise and condense magickal energy. This energy can be set into the cord itself by knotting the cords at the point of greatest concentrated effort. In other words, you concentrate on your desire and make an exclamation of the desire as you quickly make a knot (pulling it tightly as you confirm the desire). Later, untying the knot will release the desired effect. This can be helpful when working with someone who really bothers you a lot. In advance you can set the message "leave me alone" into the cord (knot) and untie it (secretly) when the person is really on your nerves. For this scenario you would simply think about the person so that you raise your emotions on the subject, then begin to loop the cord into a knot. Before pulling the cord tight into a knot, visualize the person's face. Then shout (out loud or within yourself) "Leave me alone!" Visualize the person leaving you alone as you continue for a moment to exert tension on the cord. When you next encounter the person, you are ready to release the spell.

As with all forms of magick you must be responsible when you perform a work that affects another person. Why you did something is more tied to *karmic debt* than is the act itself. For example, if you harm someone in order save another person's life, as opposed to harming someone because you seek revenge, there is a difference in the karma that you are creating for yourself. Obviously, you should seek to harm no one in the first place, but this isn't always possible.

The Components of Ritual Magick

There are essentially five so-called ingredients which contribute to the art of creating successful works of magick, or effective ritual. You can adapt these components or arrange them according to your own needs, so long as you employ them all. They are: personal will, timing, imagery, direction, and balance. Let's look at each one and gain an understanding of the concept.

The Will

This can also be thought of as motivation, temptation, or persuasion. You must be sufficiently moved enough to perform a ritual or work of magick in order to establish enough power to accomplish your goal. If you care little about the results, or put only a small amount of energy into your desire, then you are unlikely to see any real results. The stronger the need or desire, then the more likely it is that you will raise the amount of energy required to bring about the change you seek. But desire or need is not enough by itself. Remember that desire must be suppressed and the will must be focused only upon a detached view of the desired outcome of your spell or magickal rite.

Timing

In the performance of ritual magick, timing can mean success or failure. The best time to cast a spell or create a work of magick is when the target is most receptive. Receptivity is usually assured when the target is passive. People sleep, corporations close overnight and on holidays, etc. One must also take into account the phase of the moon and the season of the year. Wiccans always work with Nature and not against Her. Generally speaking 4 A.M. in the target zone area is the most effective time to cast a spell of influence over a person or a situation.

Imagery

The success of any work also depends on images created by the mind. This is where the imagination enters into the formula. Anything which serves to intensify the emotions will contribute to success. Any drawing, statue, photo, scent, article of clothing, sound, or situation that helps to merge you with your desire will greatly add to your success. Imagery is a constant reminder of what you wish to attract or accomplish. It acts as a homing device in its role as a representation of the object, person, or situation for which the spell is intended. Imagery can be shaped and directed according to the will of the Wiccan. This becomes the pattern or formula which leads to realization of desire. Surround yourself with images of your desire and you will resonate the vibrations that will attract the thing you desire.

Direction

Once enough energy has been raised, you must direct it toward your desire. Do not be anxious concerning the results, because anxiety will act to draw the energy back to you before it can take effect. Reflecting back on the spell tends to ground the energy because it draws the images and concepts back to you. Try to give the matter no more thought so as not to deplete its effectiveness. Mark a seven-day period off on your calendar and evaluate the situation seven days later. It usually takes about seven days for magick to manifest (one lunar quarter).

Balance

The last aspect of magick one has to take into account is personal balance. This means that one must consider the need for the work of magick and the consequences on both the spellcaster and the target. If anger motivates your magickal work, then wait a few hours, or sleep on it overnight. While anger can be a useful propellant for a spell, it can also cloud the thinking. If possible, make sure you have exhausted the normal means of dealing with something before you move on to a magickal solution. Make sure you are feeling well enough to work magick and plan to rest afterward. Magick requires a portion of your vital essence drawn from your aura. Replenish this with rest, even if you do not feel tired. Health problems begin in the aura long before the body is aware of them.

The Tides of Power

There are certain *tides of power* within the *magnetic field* and the ionosphere of the Earth that aid us in all of our works of magick. The stars, sun, planets, and the moon radiate their influence on us through the magnetic sphere of the Earth. In Eastern Occultism these tides are called the Tattvic Tides, and the medium through which they flow is called Prana. This is the substance just above Terrestrial Matter, known as Etheric Matter, of which there are two kinds: *Free Ether* and *Bound Ether.* Free Ether is the field that surrounds the sun, through which pass the Earth and other planets within its sphere of influence. Bound Ether surrounds the Earth itself (or any planetary body) and may be called the magnetic sphere.

As the Earth orbits the Sun, revolving on its axis as it does so, centers of stress occur in the magnetic sphere of the Earth. As a result there is a positive current of energy flowing from the East to the West, and a magnetic current passing from North to South during six months of the year (which reverses for the remaining six months). The "positive" currents emanate from the northern center, and the "negative" from the southern center. The Winter Solstice marks the beginning of the positive current which reverses after the Summer Solstice to negative. These currents of energy are marked by the Seasonal Rites occurring at the Solstices and Equinoxes (see illustrations, page 137). The terms "positive" and "negative" refer to electrical and magnetic energies of an etheric nature, as well as to those energies which we might call "waxing" and "waning."

The Equinoxes mark the periods when the daylight and darkness are of equal duration. We call this the balance of the powers of Light and Darkness. The Spring Equinox marks the time of planting. What we plant in the Spring Equinox we shall harvest by the time of the Autumn Equinox. Therefore we should look to our plans and projects and prepare works of magick intended to put us well on our way in the Path we wish to walk. Careful and detailed plans should be laid out and worked toward. The fact that the powers of Light and

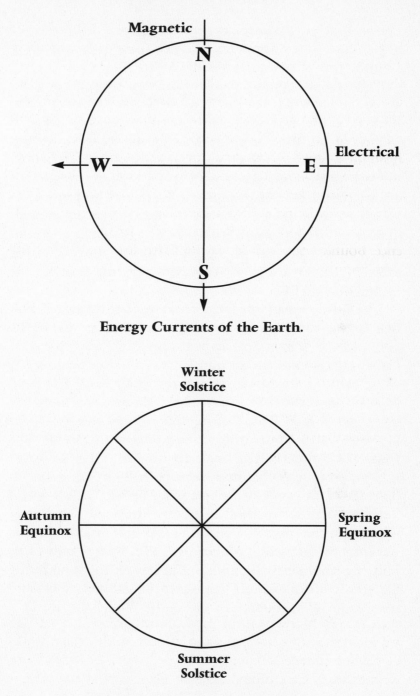

Magnetic

N

W — E — Electrical

S

Energy Currents of the Earth.

Winter
Solstice

Autumn
Equinox

Spring
Equinox

Summer
Solstice

Seasonal Currents of the Earth.

Darkness are in balance during an Equinox stabilizes our magick and allows us to create magick without encountering an imbalance of one energy or the other.

The Autumn Equinox is a time to assess our gains or losses as the time of harvest arrives. What we worked for, or failed to work for, at the time of the Spring Equinox has now come to fullness. It is a time now for choosing the seeds we wish to plant, or replant, and to create magickal spells which will be the newly sprouting seeds next Spring. Self-examination is essential at the time of the Autumn Equinox. This provides us an opportunity to identify what we need to cast off in order to advance in our spirituality. These things should be identified, sigilized, burned in the cauldron, and buried in the earth. In this way the season of decline will help what is detrimental to our higher nature ebb away.

The Solstices mark the longest and shortest periods of sunlight in the year. The Summer Solstice is the longest day of the year and the Winter Solstice is the shortest. The powers of Light and Darkness are in imbalance. This is marked by the ritual battle of the Oak King and the Holly King. The Summer Solstice is the time to pay particular attention to important matters in one's life. Blessings upon loved ones and spells of protection and nurturing are best done at this season. The fruits and flowers of our labors are now in full array before us. The promise of Nature is seen both in actuality and in potential. This is one of the reasons why the Otherworld is known as the Summerland in Wiccan theology. The Winter Solstice is the time for planning Spring magick. In the Autumn we assessed and discarded. The Winter calls to us now to plan for new projects and to correct the mistakes we have made. Spells of peace, forgiveness of self and others, and restoration are in good order during the Winter Solstice.

Chapter Nine

Lunar and Solar Consciousness

*In a magickal sense, human
consciousness can be divided into either
a lunar or solar consciousness. Solar
consciousness is by nature linear and
analytical. By comparison, lunar
consciousness is more abstract and
non-linear.*

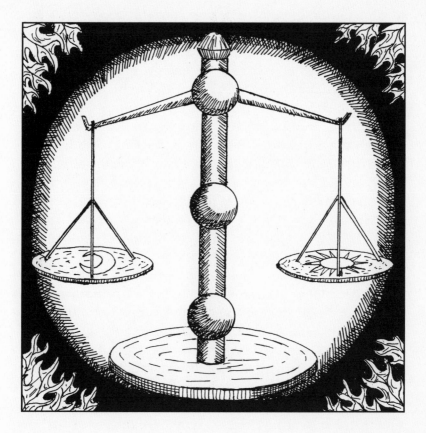

Before examining the concepts discussed in this chapter it is important to understand the definitions of the words employed here in an occult sense. I will be using such words as *masculine* and *feminine, electrical* and *magnetic, active* and *receptive,* all in context with what might appear to be gender-related issues. Please understand that I am speaking only of types of energy and states of consciousness. Therefore, when I speak of feminine energy I am not speaking of gender per se. All of the energies and states of consciousness discussed here are present to varying degrees in both men and women.

From an occult perspective, feminine energy is any force that is receptive and masculine energy is any force that is active. Masculine energy is electrical and active, feminine energy is magnetic and receptive. For our purposes active means penetrating, motivating, or stimulating. Receptive means accommodating, nurturing, or attracting. Traditionally, occultists regard the masculine polarity of energy as active on the Physical Plane and receptive on the Mental Plane. The feminine polarity is receptive on the Physical Plane and active on the Mental Plane. The elements of masculine and feminine polarities play a vital role in the function of human consciousness within the Physical Plane.

In a magickal sense, human consciousness can be divided into either a lunar or solar consciousness. Solar consciousness is by nature linear and analytical. By comparison, lunar consciousness is more abstract and non-linear. Solar magickal systems generally employ a type of magick that is direct and persuasive by force. Lunar magick tends to work behind the scenes and is quietly penetrating. In some ways lunar magick is not unlike an invasive mist. Its persuasion is more akin to seduction than it is to brute force. We symbolize the masculine energies by the bright hot light of the sun. Feminine energies are symbolized by the subtle cool light of the moon. It is important to remember that we are not talking about gender, but rather about aspects of occult consciousness.

The differences between the two aspects of occult consciousness can be connected to patriarchal versus matriarchal perspectives. Masculine mentality and energy is generally more directly controlling while the feminine counterparts are more persuasive from behind the scenes. Patriarchal religions and magickal systems are generally more "by the letter of the law" while matriarchal systems are typically more "by the spirit of the law." Naturally there are exceptions to every rule. When we generalize we cannot include all of the possibilities and we can be unfair to those who differ from the majority.

Wicca is a lunar-based Earth religion whose practices are aligned with the seasons of our planet and with the energies that flow from the various phases of the moon. In a magickal sense it differs from those religions that evolved in a *solar consciousness* because it is less ceremonial by comparison. The solar traditions generally place a higher emphasis on strict ritual guidelines and preparations. Although Wiccan traditions are not without ceremonial aspects, Wiccan magick can be practiced on the spot as needed with little in the way of preparation or adherence to prescribed formula.

I should clarify the last comment and add that Wiccan magick is still dependent on the same metaphysical laws that govern magick in general. Wiccans simply employ a less overt adherence to them. Where a ceremonial magician might carve a wand and place symbols on it, a Wiccan could pick up a twig in a forest and perform an ad lib act of magick on the spot. This is not to suggest any type of superiority, but simply to illustrate the different approaches to magick. Wiccans are as subject to the same laws governing phases of the moon, seasonal energies, and planetary influences as are any other group of occult practitioners.

Some Wiccans practice forms of Folk Magick that differ a great deal from what I would call *formula* magick. Folk Magick relies on what one believes is the inherent power of an object or symbol. Formula Magick relies on connections and their relationship to the source of power behind a symbol or within an object. In Folk Magick a person believes that simply carrying a certain herb will grant him or her some specified power. This is not unlike carrying a rabbit's foot for good luck. Such things are usually not considered dependent on the seasons or cycles of Nature. In this book we are not dealing with Folk Magick, but rather with the inner secrets behind how such things work.

From a Wiccan perspective, magick begins in the mind. At the core of the mind is the inner Self. Wiccan thought conceives of the Self as being composed of three basic levels: the

Lower Self, Middle Self, and Higher Self. The Lower Self is connected with the Physical Plane and is concerned with existence on a material level. The Middle Self is connected with the Mental Plane and is concerned with concepts and ideals on a spiritual level. The Higher Self is connected to the Divine Plane and is concerned with spirituality and rapport with deity.

Another way of viewing these aspects of Self is to picture the Lower Self as that part of us that labors and sees to our physical needs. The Middle Self is who we are, separate from our careers and social obligations. The Higher Self is that part of us that we might call our ideal image in this life. The Higher Self is directly connected to the emanation of Divinity, and can guide the Middle and Lower Selves by channeling the *Divine Will* downward through the other levels. In this way we can come to know our divine nature dwelling in rapport with the Source of All Things.

The power of the Wiccan arises from the knowledge and experience that all things are interrelated. Magickal forces and states of consciousness are created through a practical application of one's understanding of the harmony existing within this connectivity. By understanding the connections, their energies can be shaped and directed by an act of personal will power. Everything is seen as a manifestation of energy. Consciousness itself is viewed as energy, and by altering one's state of consciousness a person is able to pass from one dimension or state of existence to another. He or she can do this by mentally merging with the desired state of consciousness. Once you become like the thing you desire, then you exist in that dimension or state of being. Here you attract the inherent energies where, in occult terms, *like attracts like*.

Participation in the ways of Wiccan religion places one within the energy flow of the cycles of Nature. The inner knowledge of Nature and the mechanism of the Supernatural arises from the Wiccan's own sense of connection with the forces of Nature. In Wiccan Magick everything can be seen through metaphors. As awareness changes with increased states of consciousness, the metaphors change as well. By realizing that you are the microcosm, you arrive at the center of the macrocosm surrounding you. Each connection you make from there to the greater patterns outside of you serves as a signpost, directing the perceived path ahead. The search for ultimate truth is the reverse of searching for one's roots—one is a beginning, the other is a transition. Transition is the craft of Wiccan Magick.

The Lunar Mind

As we noted earlier, lunar consciousness is nonlinear. It is connected with the subconscious mind, which thinks and communicates in terms of images and concepts. In dreams we can be riding in a car, which becomes a bicycle, and perhaps we may not take particular notice. This is because, to the lunar mind, *travel* is the concept here. The means by which we are made mobile is secondary, and therefore the *message* always takes precedence over the *messenger.* Everything in lunar thinking is only incidental to the concept being communicated. There is no need for chronological order because only the message is important and not the means by which it was delivered. I am not talking here about dream analysis or psychology. I am talking about lunar consciousness and its use of symbols in a magickal sense.

I am not saying that the symbolism used in dreams, or by the subconscious mind for communication, is unimportant. I am saying that the message supersedes the symbols. The subconscious mind can shift symbolism in mid-communication and employ even seemingly unrelated symbols to the current theme of the dream in order to relay its intent. When we are awake it is difficult sometimes for the conscious mind to make sense of the dream. From an occult perspective, subconscious communication is not meant entirely for the conscious mind, but rather (in part) for the indwelling spirit. The conscious mind is only half of our awareness. The subconscious mind is the other half, yet we behave as though the conscious mind is fully *ourselves*.

Just as the conscious mind has at its disposal the senses through which it can discern its environment, so too does the subconscious mind. We call these senses extrasensory or psychic senses. The subconscious mind maintains an awareness while the conscious mind is fully active and dominant. The same is true of the conscious mind while we sleep. This is evidenced by our waking up in the middle of the night to potential dangers around us. Therefore when we are awake our psychic senses are operating in the background while our physical senses are dealing with the environment around us. If we allow them to interrupt our conscious processes we can employ them in a conscious mode. This can be exhausting, just as allowing our conscious mind to interrupt our subconscious mind throughout the night can leave us exhausted, come morning.

When we imitate the natural environment of the subconscious mind (the sleep state), our extrasensory abilities become more accessible to conscious influence. This is why states of relaxation or trance tend to be best for psychic consciousness.

In dream control (a method of establishing the conscious mind in the astral body) we simply do the opposite. We leave a conscious suggestion such as: *I will look at my right hand when I am dreaming,* and thus we are introducing something conscious into the state of subconscious (not unlike post-hypnotic suggestion). This is how we can operate as conscious beings while being within the astral realms. Our consciousness is introduced into our astral bodies because we have impregnated a dream state with the conscious mind instead of allowing the subconscious mind full dominance. Without doing this, astral experiences can often be mistaken for dreams.

The Solar Mind

When I spoke earlier of solar consciousness I said that it was linear and analytical. In a dream in which the car turns into a bicycle, the conscious mind will later object. It wants a reason and a connection, it wants a chronological order. Fortunately the human brain is composed of two spheres that govern different modes of consciousness. You may have heard of right sphere and left sphere consciousness with which the mind can be both analytical and abstract in its processing of information. This allows the conscious mind the ability to find meaning where none is apparent. The subconscious mind does exactly the opposite; it has the ability to be unapparent where there is meaning. Therefore its symbols can appear not to relate to the context in which they are employed.

The conscious mind is responsible for the needs of our body. The subconscious mind sees to the needs of our spirit. The two are intimately connected, as long as we have the breath of life within us, so it is important to allow each its duties. Both modes of consciousness keep us in balance when they operate in a healthy manner. To give over completely to lunar consciousness is to become disconnected to reality as expressed in human society. To give over totally to solar consciousness is to lose connection with spiritual reality as expressed in human religion. Thus the conscious mind is also known as the guardian. It protects us from slipping back into the natural mentality of our spirits as they existed prior to our incarnation within the physical dimension.

Solar consciousness allows us to investigate with a balanced perspective not only the physical world but also the metaphysical world. It is a tool of our whole consciousness, employed to break concepts down into finite elements that can be independently examined. Once examined they can be pieced back together, revealing the hidden meaning and use of the concept. Without the conscious mind we would operate in a microcosm where there was no meaning, and everything would be seemingly disconnected experiences without meaning or purpose.

In a magickal sense the solar mind sees the connections between the phases of the moon and the cycles of the seasons. It understands the interactions of the Elemental and Astral Realms. It allows us to act on these forces whereby we can work our magick. What it lacks is the ability to experience these things, for these are all experiences of the lunar mind. Therefore it gives us a boost so that we can reach a higher realm.

The Magickal Mind

When solar and lunar consciousness unite, they produce the magickal consciousness. Thus we have the conceptual mind directed by the analytical mind, and together both are more powerful than the sum of their parts. We can see the value of conscious unification with the subconscious in such a field as biofeedback. Here the conscious mind directs the subconscious to manifest a directed state of consciousness. The important thing to note here is that this is a relationship and not a domination.

The magickal mind is the doorway to and from the Collective Consciousness of our race. The subconscious mind is the gateway to the Astral Plane. This inner sphere of our mind is where magick arises and is made a functional part of our consciousness as a whole. Images arise as hidden symbolism and are given form under the direction of the conscious mind. These forms then become empowered as conscious symbols and pass through the subconscious mind out into the etheric substance from which dreams are fashioned.

In occult philosophy everything is connected and interrelated. Portals to and from the other worlds are opened by the energy of altered states of consciousness. The solar mind opens such portals by evoking entities dwelling in other dimensions, and uses their power to access these mystical realms. The lunar mind uses its own frequency, or natural alignment with nonphysical states of existence, and thus acts as a conduit through which condensed images can pass into astral material and become manifest.

Meditative states of consciousness are conducive to accessing psychic and magickal levels of the mind. Here we allow the subconscious mind to establish itself in the conscious domain. Essentially this is the reverse process of the dream control method. When we unite the conscious and subconscious minds we can create an image, condense and empower it through concentration of the will, and then plant it in the subconscious mind by symbolizing it. Once it becomes a symbol we need no longer think about it as a concept or a desire. By transferring the symbol we can plant the magickal seed within the subconscious realm. This is important, because the conscious mind will keep the concept bound to the physical plane if we allow it to keep thinking about the desired outcome.

The subconscious part of the magickal mind is directly linked to the Elemental Plane or Plane of Forces (see chapter five). Anything released to the subconscious mind will flow into the astral levels. When the conscious mind intentionally symbolizes a desire and passes it to the subconscious then its power is sufficient to evoke a response from the Astral Light. Astral material will form around the symbolized concept and create a magickal thought-form. There must be, of course, a source of energy involved in establishing the symbolized desire to begin with. For further information, please refer to chapters five, six, and seven.

The Magickal Personality

A very important aspect of solar and lunar consciousness is the magickal personality. This is the persona that a Wiccan takes on in order to tap the deepest resources of his or her magickal abilities. The ability to access supernatural power for one's own purposes is the greatest secret of the magickal art. To accomplish this, one can employ a magickally created personality that represents the Adept or Magus within. Though related to the multiple personality of the psychological realm, this is a controllable mental entity. It presents itself and withdraws by conscious will on the part of the dominant personality already in place.

To create the magickal personality you must mentally establish it through meditations focused on the Triad of Power: *Wisdom, Compassion,* and *Power.* These three elements are the sign of the spiritual follower of the Magickal Path. To possess power balanced by compassion and governed by wisdom is the only safe use of occult abilities. This teaching (among others) is preserved in the Caduceus symbol. The twin serpents touch in three places on the rod, marking off each element of magickal consciousness. We call these the *Triadic Elements* of the magickal consciousness.

To begin building the personality you must first obtain a new, unused ring. Choose one that is symbolic of magickal power to you, perhaps bearing a pentagram or other mystical symbol. In addition decide on a magickal name for your new persona. Then you will need to meditate on each of the Triadic Elements individually. Begin with power and see in your mind's eye the power you wish to wield. After creating a daydream-type image it is time to fix the image with something like the following words:

For Power

I call upon the Source of All Things
to instill within me the power of magick
through which I can draw down the moon,
call upon the gods,
and manifest my desire in accordance with my will.

For Compassion

I call upon the Source of All Things
to instill within me the awareness called compassion
through which I can discern true will,

call upon my Higher Nature,
and manifest my desire with harm to none.

For Wisdom

I call upon the Source of All Things
to instill within me the wisdom of forethought
through which I may harm no one,
call upon my experience,
and manifest my desire to know, dare, will, and keep silent.

The next step is to visualize a silvery mist forming behind you. Then imagine a hooded, robed figure, exactly your size, appearing through the mist so that it comes to stand directly behind you. At this point slip on your magick ring and mentally see the robed figure merge into your body. Once this is firm in your mind, you will need to create the alignment with words like the following:

I am (name) *born of power, compassion, and wisdom.*
Though born of this world, my race is of the stars.
With harm to none I manifest my will
and submit to my Higher Self;
To know, to dare, to will and to be silent.

The next stage is very important. Visualize the silver mist forming behind you. Slowly begin to slip off the ring. As you do so, visualize the robed figure separating from you, moving back into the mist. As the ring leaves your finger, mentally see the figure disappear into the mist. Visualize the mist fading away and then look around you, confirming that everything is normal in your surroundings. From this point on, the magickal personality must only be allowed to come when you call it in the manner described here. Allow it to merge with you only when you are performing spells or ritual magick. Then have it exit into the mist once you have finished.

Eventually the magickal personality will appear in the mist when you need it, as in times of psychic or magickal attack. It is still important that you consciously allow it to merge at such times. Never let it enter you on its own accord. If it does, use the ring removal method to dismiss it. Once you have worked with the personality a few times you will understand the power you have over it and the ways in which it can behave. In any and all cases you must remain fully in control of the magickal personality. Never allow it to be the dominant personality.

Light and Darkness

When we speak of Light and Darkness we are not referring to good and evil. Modern Wiccans do not personify these forces or acknowledge a conscious force of good or evil per se. Good and evil are more or less seen as personal perspectives. However, in life we certainly all experience cycles of gain and loss, pain and pleasure, sense and nonsense. The debate lies in whether such things are random occurrences, pre-established patterns, or conscious/subconscious influences.

It is a metaphysical principle that there is a duality to all things. In an occult sense we say that there are forces of *Light* and forces of *Darkness.* Light shows us the way and reveals the Path ahead. Darkness presents obstacles through which we gain experience, strength, and wisdom. We do not associate Light with the day or Darkness with the night. Likewise we do not equate Darkness with lunar forces or Light with solar forces. We speak instead of spiritual energies and states of consciousness.

From such a perspective we can view the gods and goddesses of our Mythology as personifications of the forces of Light and Darkness. In these tales we can see the interaction of such forces from the primal consciousness of our ancient ancestors. It is important to maintain the old connections and to integrate them with modern perspectives. Through joining old and new consciousness we can bring balance to our understanding of the mysteries around us.

Wiccans seek balance in all things. Therefore, to walk in balance we must acknowledge and accept the forces of Light and Darkness in our lives. Each is a teacher in its own right, and through them we learn perspective and discernment. To focus exclusively on either Light or Darkness is equally deceptive to our consciousness. Light provides us with knowledge, but it is from Darkness that we draw wisdom. In Light we see clearly and can discern with the mind. In Darkness we experience the pain and strife that are catalysts to the wisdom of their avoidance.

Introverts and people who have been subject to trauma tend to be more psychic on a receptive level than those who do not fit into these categories. Our psychic nature lies within the magickal mind, which is shaped by the powers of Light and Darkness. The Sage or Magus sees both as blessings in his or her life. Knowing that everything is cyclical, he or she does not despair in the Darkness or fail to be prepared in the Light. This gives us a balanced magickal consciousness that helps us walk the middle path of lasting peace.

Chapter Ten

Understanding
Wiccan Rites

*Wiccan rites usually begin with the
intention of creating a sacred space in
which to offer devotions to one's deities or
to perform works of magick.*

R itual magick is a form of symbolic communication on both the physical and spiritual levels. This communication is capable of opening up portals to other dimensions as well as initiating altered states of consciousness/subconsciousness. Each symbol, gesture, or action corresponds to a concept and serves as a catalyst by which the hidden principle can be activated. The principle itself is connected to the thought-form of any given concept. A concept formed by the magickal will of the Wiccan stimulates the Astral Light. Every action creates an energy that in turn causes the Astral Light to react. The traditional correspondences of ritual magick are pre-established, along with time-proven methods of obtaining specifically desired results.

Creating the Sacred Circle

Wiccan rites usually begin with the intention of creating a sacred space in which to offer devotions to one's deities or to perform works of magick. The first act is to cleanse the area by sweeping and then sprinkling salt water around the circle. Then the circle can be laid out with a rope or a circle of stones or flowers to mark the perimeter. White candles are set at each quarter of the circle marking the north, east, south, and west. Once this is accomplished, the altar can be prepared. The altar serves as a focal point and a *battery* from which to draw energy as the ritual proceeds.

In most Mystery Traditions the altar is oriented to the north quarter of the ritual setting. Some modern Witches orient the altar to the east quarter. The north is considered the place of power and the ritual work is usually oriented to this quarter. Therefore, in traditions originating from older practices, everyone is basically facing north as they orient to the altar. Traditionally the altar is round, but a rectangle or square table may be used instead. Laying out the altar is an important part of any ritual and should be performed with concentration on the inner meaning of each item as it is placed. Bear in mind that as you set up an altar and cast a circle you are creating your own microcosm of the Universe (from which you will create your own reality). Once established, the ritual circle is a Wiccan's temple.

In accordance with the Inner Teachings, a black cloth is laid over the table to symbolize the darkness of procreation from which all things manifest. Black absorbs all light and in this context black then possesses the attributes of the full spectrum of Divine Light. The goddess and god candles are placed to the northernmost part of the altar; the goddess candle is set

to the northwest and the god candle to the northeast. Icons of
the Goddess and God are placed next to the candles and face
south. This represents their presence as they oversee the
process of creation that you are setting in motion.

The altar pentacle is then placed on the center of the altar
to mark the focal point of the rite. In other words, it represents the physical plane at the point where it intersects with
the spiritual elements. Then elemental bowls are placed
around the pentacle, representing the creative materials from
which all things are made manifest. The bowl representing
Earth is set in the north position and contains soil or peb-
bles. To the east set a bowl containing incense (smoking) to
represent Air. At the south end of the pentacle set a bowl
with a votive candle for Fire. Finally, to the west place a bowl
with purified Water. This act symbolizes the four elements
coming into harmony through which manifestation can
now be directed.

Now it is time to place the ritual tools. The ritual wand is
set on the altar next to the Air Elemental bowl and pointing
north. The athame is placed to the south beneath the votive
candle and pointing west. The chalice is set to the west by the
Elemental bowl of Water. With this arrangement the altar is
now complete. Mundane tools may also be placed now, such as
a utility knife, candle snuffer, and so on. It is not important
where these mundane items are placed, so feel free to let your
own tastes dictate the arrangement.

Now that the altar is set up, the ritual circle can be cast.
Casting a circle typically involves several steps:

1. Charging the athame or sword
2. Tracing out the ritual circle perimeter
3. Evoking the Elementals
4. Evoking the Watchers
5. Declaring the circle cast.

To begin you will want to charge the blade with which you are about to cast the circle. Touch the tip of the blade into each of the Elemental bowls on the altar, beginning at the north and moving clockwise, and declare:

I charge this blade by the Elemental of _____."

In most traditions the correspondences will be Earth—north, Air—east, Fire—south, and Water—west. Then present the blade in a salute-like fashion to the altar image of the Goddess and then to the God. Hold the blade pointing north and say:

Strict watch and charge I give Thee, that by your power no evil thing approach or enter in.

Take the blade and, beginning at the north quarter, tread the circle clockwise, tracing out the perimeter line by pointing the tip of the blade downward. Visualize a stream of energy pouring outward from you through the blade and into the circle. In most traditions an evocation is spoken during the circle casting to confirm the act being performed. The most traditional one is:

I conjure thee, O' Circle of power that thou beest a boundary between the world of men and the realms of the Mighty Ones, a guardian and protection that shall preserve and contain the power that I raise with thee. Wherefore do I bless Thee and consecrate Thee.

At this stage the circle is again sprinkled with salt water. Then, beginning at the north quarter, light the circle candle and say words to this effect:

I call upon you spirits of Earth to gather at this circle and ask for the blessings of your presence which will impart to this sacred space your emanation of power.

Light each circle candle in turn, moving clockwise, and repeat these words addressing the appropriate element as you do so. When you have finished this the circle will bear an elemental blessing and it is then time to call on the Watchers.

Beginning again at the north and moving clockwise to each quarter you will trace out a pentagram in the air using the appropriate quarter candle. Lift the candle above your head, pointing north, and trace out a five-pointed star, moving in a clockwise pattern and returning to the overhead position. To do so you will move your hand downward to about right hip level and then upward toward your left shoulder, across to your right shoulder, downward to your left hip, and then back to above your head. In many traditions the athame is used in place of the candle. As you trace the pentagram you will want to speak an evocation addressing each quarter Watcher with words to this effect:

> *By the power of the Wiccan's Craft and in the names of the Great Goddess and God, I summon Thee, O' Watcher of the* (name of quarter) *to bear witness to this rite and to guard and protect all within this sacred circle.*

Repeat this at each quarter, moving from the north in a clockwise movement, and returning north.

At this stage you have now completed the basic casting of a ritual circle. All that is left now is to return to the altar, face north, rap the handle of your athame on the pentacle three times and say:

> *By the Craft of my magick and by witness of the four Watchers, I now declare this circle to be properly cast.*

From this point you can now proceed with seasonal rites or Initiations, works of magick, and so forth. When you have completed the ritual you will need to dissolve the circle.

Beginning at the north quarter, take the quarter candle and trace out the pentagram in reverse order, starting at the above head position but moving counterclockwise this time. Recite words to this effect as you do so:

Hear me Old Ones, I honor You for Your attendance and bid
You depart now in peace to your secret Realms. With love I say
Hail and Farewell.

Repeat the above action at each of the quarters (moving
west, south, east, and north again).

Point the athame blade down toward the circle and tread
the same counterclockwise direction, mentally drawing the
power back up through your blade from the circle perimeter. Once the circle has been tread in full reverse return to
the altar. Rap the handle three times on the altar pentacle
and declare the circle to be dissolved. Extinguish all quarter
candles and all other ritual flames, and the circle will be
fully dissolved.

Concerning Tools and Ritual Paraphernalia

If one looks closely at the tools of the Craft it is easy to see
that they resemble the weapons of a Knight. The tools I am
referring to are the Blade, Chalice, Wand, and Pentacle. These
are the traditional tools of Western Occultism which we first
find depicted together on the Magician card of the Italian
Tarot during the fifteenth century. The Wiccan's blade is
called an athame and is symbolic of a Knight's sword. The
wand is a lance, the chalice is a helmet (turned upside down)
and the pentacle is a shield. These Craft tools are the "weapons"
of a spiritual warrior, or a priest or priestess.

The cords of initiation typically worn around the Wiccan's
waist are remnants of the bindings which once held the Sacrificial King/Slain God. They mark an individual as a member
of this ancient mystery tradition. The altar is symbolic of the
portal that is the tomb, the Gateway to other Realms. In the
Neolithic Cult of the Dead we find burial mounds with small
openings that are believed to be portals for the departed spirit. These later appear throughout Europe as Fairy Mounds.

My earlier book *The Wiccan Mysteries* (Llewellyn, 1997) goes into this in greater depth, should you be interested in further information.

The ritual circle represents the unbroken Cycle of the year, which is at the heart of The Old Religion. The Watchtowers placed at the four quarters of the ritual circle are associated with the four Elements of Earth, Air, Fire, and Water. The Elemental quarters represent the portals to the higher Realms that lay beyond this World. The Watchers themselves represent the "awareness" of our Path as it is imprinted on the planes (*watched*, so to speak) and thus are connected to the Akashic Records mentioned in chapter six. There are many other such associations and connections too numerous to include in this single chapter.

The use of cakes and wine in Wiccan ceremonies dates back to ancient times and is connected to an Occult Mystery Tradition. This is the Tradition of the Divine Sacrificial King/ Slain God, who is often called the Harvest Lord. Because the survival of early humankind depended on the fertility of animals, crops, and themselves, fertility itself became the basis for the early cult focus. Fertility leads to birth, the portal into the physical world from an outer invisible world connected to our material dimension. The nature of the one who is coming through this portal (why they came and what their purpose is) depends on breeding.

Breeding (selective reproductive strains) was learned by the early humans from observing and experimenting with animals and plants. They easily observed that the "best" produced the best, and that many of the desired traits could be passed on if the breeding was controlled. Death was seen as an exit from this world, just as birth had been an entrance. It seemed logical to assume that the one who died was returning to where he or she had been before they were born. Death was thus seen as migration.

In the *Other World* the sacrificial messenger was *delivered* to the gods to speak on behalf of the Clan's needs. It was also believed that this person would return to the Clan as a "Savior," help deliver them from the problems of this World, and secure a place for them in the next world. This is why in the Descent of the Goddess (Myth) we read:

> *...you must return again at the same time and at the same place as the loved ones. And you must meet, and know, and remember, and love them again....*

This is the major rendering of this passage, but there is another. In the Descent Myth we find a passage referring to the *"three great mysteries in the Life of Man."* These mysteries are also connected to the Divine Sacrificial King Mythos. The three great mysteries are Birth, Death, and Rebirth. The Descent Myth tells us that *"love controls them all."* The Myth goes on to say:

> *... but to be reborn, you must die, and be made ready for a new body. And to die you must be born, and without love, you may not be born.*

This was, in part, instructional for the person who was being sacrificed, but it also pertained to the populace as a whole. Without the bonds of love between this world and the next there can be no interaction—either between individuals or gods. This Mythos is also connected with that of the Hanged Man (who was the Hooded Man).

The Hooded Man is perhaps best personified by the Guardian of the Sacred Grove at Nemi, where he was called *Rex Nemorensis,* the King of the Woods. This enigmatic character embodies the idea of new life springing out of death. He also brings the creative power of the Tree Spirit of the Sacred Grove to the people. The Mythos of the Hooded Man can be seen in many cultures. In various parts of Europe he is known by many names: The Green Man, Jack-in-the-green, Jack-in-the-bush, Robin Goodfellow, Robyne of the Woods, and Robin o' the Hood. The position known as the Hanged Man originates from that of the Hooded Man. He is the symbol of self-sacrifice for the good of the whole. The key to under-standing the Hanged Man lies in the fact that he is *enlightened* as he hangs on the tree. He has denied the Self and turned to the greater divinity within.

The title of the Hanged Man means, in an occult sense, *suspended mind*, because "man" and "mind" are from the same Sanskrit root (used by early occultists). The title refers also to the utter dependence of human personality on the Cosmic life. He hangs now as a co-worker with the Divine, having placed his own ego out of the way of the Divine inflow. Only in this way can he attain the Higher Consciousness and become useful to his people. The sacred tree of the grove represents the bridge to the other worlds. It is the Consciousness that hangs on the tree that serves to unify humankind with the Divine. It is the fruit of enlightenment.

The mental attitude suggested by the Hanged Man then is "Not my Will, but Thine," which is a very old teaching spoken by all the Avatars. This is the mentality of the Adept, and also can be said of anyone who works in a field of applied science for the greater good. The Self is an illusive, personal thing constituting really nothing more than a mask. The face behind the mask is the higher nature reflective of the source of divinity within the individual. The purpose or motive of the Cosmic Life is to teach through the Hanged Man that the true will (the maskless face) is absolutely free and certain to be realized.

The foundation I am trying to lay here is that of the willing sacrifice. If we go back far enough in human history we will find human sacrifice. It is nothing to be proud of certainly, but it is nothing to hide from either. In earlier chapters I explained why this practice was performed. What I did not address fully was how the sacrificed body was used. Because he was considered to be descended from other Divine Kings (the breeding I spoke of), it was believed that the flesh and blood of the Slain God contained mystical properties. Therefore small bits of his flesh were distributed to the Clan, and diluted portions of his blood were consumed. In this way, the Clan was connected to his divine nature.

In time animal sacrifice replaced human sacrifice, and later still plants served as the Slain God, but the practice of consuming the Slain God never changed. Today it is still performed in the ritual of cakes and wine that represent the body and the blood of the Slain God (now Lord of the Harvest). In some Traditions the cakes symbolize the God and the wine symbolizes the Goddess (that is, their "essence"). This is all part of the Mystery Tradition, and goes deeply to our very core as members of a Clan, a race, a people, or a nation.

In the Autumn Equinox Rite, as practiced by followers of the Old Ways, a Mystery Play is performed in which the Divine Victim is symbolically slain. A representation of a skull is used at this rite, symbolizing the former Divine Victim. A token of fluid of the life essence of the new "King" is obtained and mixed with a token portion of fluid from the High Priestess. This is placed in a bag and buried in a sacred garden where ritual plants are grown. Originally it would have hung in the forest on a tree to provide for a plentiful hunt, or been buried in a cultivated field for abundant crops. Today we offer it up for the needs of our Clan, whatever they may happen to be at the time.

In ancient times the Divine Victim was cut up into pieces and given to the soil. Small portions of his flesh and his blood were incorporated into a *communion* meal and given to the Priest(ess)hood to distribute. Today we symbolically perform this ancient rite with the ceremony of cakes and wine. The sacrifice comes from the Plant Kingdom, but the human connection is still there and the ancient current still flows through the ceremony. As humans evolved spiritually, so too did their practices, but nothing is ever forgotten.

Being of the Blood

It was once believed that certain individuals, royalty, or other spiritual leaders were actually descended from the "gods" (or in some cases from non-human races such as the Elven or Fay). It is obvious from this that their blood was held to be very precious, since they were considered to be *Demi-gods.* Because they represented the spiritual base power of the Clan it was important to preserve the purity of their bloodline and to ensure that it was passed along through the generations. In those early times it was taught that the gifts of psychic abilities were maintained and transmitted by a direct blood link with the priestesshood or priesthood (who were themselves either direct descendants by bloodline, or were indirect by virtue of having received the royal blood). This is one reason why the Church ordered the slaying of whole families of Witches during the Inquisition, hoping to destroy the ancient bloodlines. Witches were very often associated with Fairies and other nonhuman races, and were portrayed as different from humans in many European folklore tales.

Symbolically, anyone who drank of the blood of one of these descendants was said to be *of the blood* and could in turn pass on the blood through ritual communion of the wine and cakes (which were anointed with the royal blood of either a direct descendant or indirect blood receiver). As the Old Religion grew, anyone who was born into the family of those who had been of the blood were considered to be also of the blood. This was the basic significance of being "hereditary" (along with being reborn among those whom one had known and loved before).

Initiation

The issue of initiation in Wicca is a very hotly debated subject that raises many questions. What is initiation really, and can people perform it for themselves, or does it require someone who has passed through the process already? Is initiation even necessary in order for people to call themselves Wiccans? Is initiation a magical transformation, an astral alignment, a symbolic act, or simply a personal commitment to follow a chosen path? Is there any practical difference between being initiated into a social club (fraternity/sorority, etc.) and being initiated into Wicca?

If you look up the word "initiation" in a dictionary you will find a definition of this sort: *"an initiating or being initiated; the ceremony by which a person is initiated into a fraternity, etc.,"* and of the word "initiate" you will find the definition: *"to admit as a member into a fraternity, club, etc."*

The word itself comes from the Latin *initiatus* meaning "to enter upon." In everyday language the word can mean a mundane ceremony such as in joining a local club or organization. In mystical and occult communities the term "initiation" has long been understood to mean the passing on of occult powers and knowledge, a transformation or realignment of the person and his or her relationship with Deity, Self, and the Universe (macrocosm and microcosm together).

In modern Wicca the meaning of initiation has changed to include a concept known as *self-initiation.* In effect, this is a self-proclamation before one's deities as to one's desire to follow the ways of Wicca. The entire subject of initiation is a very sensitive topic among Wiccans, as there are those who feel that initiation can only be bestowed by someone already possessing the knowledge desired by the Neophyte. It is not my belief that this issue can be fully resolved here or anywhere else, but I do feel as though we all need to look at both sides of the debate. So just what is initiation, and how do we come to an understanding of not only its definition but its intended purpose as well?

Dion Fortune, a one-time member of The Golden Dawn and recognized as one of the most important persons in twentieth-century occultism, wrote two texts in particular that deal with the subject of initiation, *The Esoteric Orders and Their Work*[1] and *The Training and Work of an Initiate.*[2] In the first

---

1   Fortune, Dion. *The Esoteric Orders and Their Work* (Wellingborough: The Aquarian Press, 1982), pp. 139–142.

2   Fortune, Dion. *The Training and Work of an Initiate* (Wellingborough: The Aquarian Press, 1972), pp. 25–41.

book she writes: *"Many would-be initiates make the mistake of thinking that the will to initiate is sufficient, but this is not the case."* In this same text she outlines the system and techniques that are applied in an initiation ceremony to bring a person through the transforming experience of initiation. She then concludes: *"This is achieved by means of ritual initiation, and the symbolism of the ritual employed is designed to carry consciousness along the appropriate association-chain."*

In her works Dion Fortune covers the ancient teachings concerning mystical and magical transformations, and the Traditions of antiquity which formed the methods necessary to transmit this process to an individual. From the days of antiquity until the latter part of the twentieth century, initiation was always considered to be a mystical and magical process based on well-established metaphysical laws that were carefully and skillfully incorporated into a ritual ceremony. In the 1990s this time-proven concept is challenged by many who teach that initiation is simply a personal commitment to follow a given path marked by an affirmation that one is a Wiccan, and that a person can *self-initiate.* In the book *Living Wicca*[3] author Scott Cunningham states:

> *Though a physical initiation isn't necessary to practice Wicca, it is a ritual statement of one's allegiance to the Craft. The initiate can, from that day forward, clearly claim that they're Wiccan....*

Cunningham argues that the time-honored act of power being transferred from the initiator to the initiate is not necessary in self-initiation because the God and Goddess themselves pass the power directly to the would-be Wiccan when sincerely asked for it. In ancient times people sought out the *masters* who had spent almost a lifetime cultivating the mystical arts. These masters possessed ritual methods through which a mentality and an astral alignment could be passed to another individual.

3   Cunningham, Scott. *Living Wicca: A Further Guide for the Solitary Practitioner.* (St. Paul: Llewellyn Publications, 1993), pp. 33–37.

In traditional initiation one who has attained a desired connection with magical abilities, spirituality, powers, or whatever passes an energy to the initiate (sometimes in conjunction with an experience or challenge of some sort). The purpose is to align the individual with those forces with which the initiator himself or herself has already achieved connection. The argument against the concept of self-initiation is that a person cannot pass to another person something which they themselves do not already possess. Likewise a person cannot give themselves something which they do not possess or already have access to. The argument in favor of self-initiation is that we all bear the divine spark of our creators within us, from which we can experience initiation directly from the center of that indwelling divine nature.

In the occult concept it is the purpose of initiation to expose an individual to a current of energy (or an experience) wherein the person is realigned, and prepared to receive and to understand the mysteries of the system into which they are entering. It has been taught that when someone is not properly prepared it is unlikely that they are going to understand what is being presented to them, nor will they progress very far without the traditional keys revealed through a knowledge of the Wiccan Mysteries.

The best argument against the necessity of an *initiator* is that if it were necessary for someone else to initiate a person, then how did the first initiates appear to begin with? Certainly no one was around to pass the power to them. This is not an unreasonable argument and to answer it we have to look at the "history/herstory" of Initiation. The pre-initiators were those individuals in early communities who had a very strong personal connection to the "inner world" of Nature, in other words with the so-called "supernatural." These were the shamans, the "medicine people." Dion Fortune refers to this type of individual in *The Training and Work of an Initiate*[4] where she writes:

---

4   Fortune, 1972, p. 26.

If we study the lives and writings of these men and women who sought to know, not merely for the sake of knowledge, but in order to apply that knowledge to the relief of human suffering, we shall be struck by the fact that these lives have many things in common, factors which mark them off from the lives of eminent men of other types. They usually have from early childhood a sense of some work which they are to do; sooner or later they find this work, and never falter in their devotion to it; and thirdly...they have a sense of being in contact with something higher than themselves which uses them as instruments for the service of their fellows.

Clearly it appears that some individuals do appear to either be endowed with, or carry with them from a previous life, a certain seemingly natural ability to connect with the *supernatural* on their own. They seem to be able to discover and connect together those things which lead to an initiate level *mentality* without the need for an external teacher (at least not a human one). This would be the occult counterpart of the *child prodigy* who masters the piano at age two. Although these individuals are rare, they do bring into question whether traditional initiation is a universal requirement.

What we have in the case of the first pre-initiators is a select group of individuals who came to (or were led to) an understanding of the spirit world and physical world, and their relationship with each other. Through much trial and error they discovered and developed the use of herbs, spirit-animal power forms, and all of those things which we commonly associate with Wicca, shamanism, and the like. In the course of time they learned a technique to pass their own alignment with these forces on to those individuals who did not already possess this ability themselves. The majority of their Clan did not possess these abilities, which is why these Sages were held in such high regard by their tribal people initially; they were special and had the power.

There are essentially three types of initiation: mundane initiation, ritual initiation, and spiritual initiation. Mundane initiation is any ceremony which is performed to mark an individual as a member of any given organization. Mundane initiations are social only, meaning that they contain no magical or mystical elements, but serve in form only. Ritual initiation is a means of creating a magical transformation and is composed of metaphysical techniques that establish the *association chain* Dion Fortune said was necessary to transform or realign the would-be initiate.

Spiritual initiation is what some people call *spontaneous initiation* and is the kind which many avatars experienced. Examples of this are Buddha becoming enlightened beneath the Bodhi tree, Jesus hearing "God" proclaim him as his son as he came up from the baptismal water in the Jordan river, etc. These are spiritual initiations because they come from a higher realm, not of this Earth. By comparison, the self-initiation ritual is more closely related to a personal dedication ritual in which a person declares his or her intention to follow a chosen path (often asking for the blessings of whatever deities might be involved). Here the person is not magically transformed or astrally aligned by traditional methods, but in many cases may experience a profound spiritual experience as the divine spark within is awakened by a new light.

In ancient times the vast majority of practitioners were not initiates but simply followers of the Craft. The initiates were the priests and priestesses who had undergone special training and had entered into the Mysteries through ritual initiation. They were respected by the people and accepted as leaders because they *had the power* and their initiation led them to the service of others within their community. Initiation was not so much for the person being initiated as it was for the people to whom the initiate would later become responsible (such as typically befalls the village healer, charm maker, or magician).

In ancient times, to be an initiate was a special thing and not necessarily desired by all practitioners of the Craft. Many were content to simply practice the Old Ways and join in the religious celebrations without the responsibilities of the

Priest(ess)hood. Today most Wiccans desire to be an initiate for many reasons, one of which is because of the ancient associations linked to the term itself. Initiation had special meaning in the old days, and initiates were respected because of what they had experienced due to the labors of their training, just as today we respect those who have labored to earn a doctorate degree or something of that nature.

If this view is an accurate one, then where does it leave the person who cannot connect with an initiator? Can he or she still practice the Craft without being initiated? Certainly any person who has a sincere desire to practice Wicca can do so without a stamp of approval by another. There are many excellent books available that can guide an individual to worship the God and Goddess, learn basic magical spells, connect with animal power spirits, learn herbal and healing arts, and so on. Not receiving initiation at the hands of another does not mean that you are not a Wiccan. It just means that you are not an initiate in the time-honored sense of the word. If you choose to let that bother you, then you have missed the point of this chapter.

For those readers who wish to practice the Craft but have no teacher/initiator, I have provided a list of suggested reading at the end of this book that I believe will be useful in helping you to establish a firm foundation for the solitary practice of Wicca. I have separated the books into categories of study in order to help you focus on any areas that you feel may need more attention than others. There is a great deal that you can learn by yourself. Think not about limitations, but rather on the power of your free will.

Ancient Rites in Modern Times

When we look at the ancient rites of our ancestors, we note an emphasis on such things as the fertility of crops and animals. Most Wiccans no longer hunt for food or plow fields for planting, or copulate in the fresh furrows to encourage an abundant crop. Despite our so-called progress as a race, our basic needs are still the same: food, shelter, safety, sex, family, love, and purpose. Today's rituals for an abundant crop are performed for the fruits that our own labors may bring. For most of us, our jobs and careers have replaced roles as hunters and farmers. Still these ancient rites address our basic needs and are not out of date in this respect.

Fertility rites once performed for the increase of Clan and livestock now address our immediate family and community needs. The essence of fertility is still required in the world because it is the very life force itself. Some Wiccans feel that fertility rites are obsolete due to the overpopulation of our planet. It is important, however, to remember that it was part of the ancient rites to help empower the soil as well as plant and animal life with the condensed energy of fertility raised within a circle of magick. The personal fertility of the Clan was secondary. In modern Wicca many Traditions have removed all of the sexual energy techniques from the rituals and replaced them with symbolic gestures. It is indeed a challenge to preserve the power of the old Traditions, yet adapt to modern circumstances without compromising the integrity of either.

The seasonal rites were designed to give energy back into the world, particularly so at the time of an Equinox or Solstice. Just as soil is depleted by crop growing and the fields must be rotated, so too is the etheric substance depleted that empowers the mechanism of life-giving force on this planet of ours. For example, at the Summer Solstice it is part of initiate rituals to raise an energy field and to impregnate it with a thought-form. Once this *cone of power* is formed, then it is released and directed into the bound ether of our community (reference chapter six). The cone can be charged to disperse pollution in the air, or to rid the community atmosphere of negativity (crimes, gangs, rapes, etc.) or to replace lost fertility in the soil. In this way we join in the dance of Nature and work in *common cause* with Her efforts to maintain positive and life-giving energies.

Each of the eight Sabbats of the year serve a similar purpose and contribute to what is appropriate at any given season of the year. The full moon rituals are likewise times of renewal and regeneration. There is an occult property to moonlight itself, and if properly drawn, condensed, impregnated, and directed it too can be used to give life back into the world. Another purpose for the rite of the full moon is to empower us as Wiccans. Moonlight can be used to increase psychic ability, and to recharge the power centers of an individual. It is from moonlight that we as Wiccans draw and renew our own power. Science is beginning to catch up a bit now with ancient occult knowledge and is taking a look at the effects of the moon upon us and our world. Soon science will begin to see (perhaps through quantum theories) that the Occult Teachings of the Craft are a metaphysical science as valid as any physical science.

As noted in chapters seven and eight, the bound ether of our planet is what Eastern Mystics call the Akasha. There is also the microcosm of the bound ether of a community such as a city or a village. This ether is the atmospheric energy that is formed by the Collective Consciousness of the people who live there. All places possess this bound ether, even bars and nightclubs, and you can *feel* it when you enter them. It affects the people who come into contact with it and over long periods of time can change the way they view things. It is the bound ether of a place that holds the images psychics can perceive about the setting.

It is part of the work we can do as Wiccans to cleanse a community of negative thought-forms. Wiccans have long been the local healers, not only of the people but also of places. Ritual magic can change the vibration of the bound ether and thus change its feel and therefore its effect. Our religion is not an anachronism, but rather a viable force for renewal and regeneration of both community and the Earth itself. The Earth is a living and conscious entity. She is growing ill from the pollution and the abuse of natural resources by government and industry. It is my personal belief that the growth in Wicca as a religion today is an answer to the call of our Mother Earth.

Chapter Eleven

Walking the
Magickal Path

The Magician card teaches us that
personal power originates from conscious
control of the forces and things that lie
within the subconscious and self-c
onscious levels. The posture of the
Magician illustrates that the energy
comes to us from above.

The Tarot card of the Magician is an interesting study for those who choose to walk the path of magick. Decks originating in different European countries depict the Magician engaged in diverse occupations. In the early Italian decks he is often a cobbler repairing shoes. In the French decks, the Magician is a juggler practicing sleight of hand tricks or playing the old shell game. As the Tarot evolved in imagery through the centuries, the Magician later appeared as a metalsmith, alchemist, merchant, and innkeeper.

The Magician is a curious figure. As a cobbler he prepares us for the walk that lies ahead. As a juggler he reveals the balance that is essential to a magickal life. In the character of the sleight of hand artist he teaches us that things are not always as they appear to be. The metalsmith and alchemist speak to us of transformation, which is the true Craft of the Magician. In the last image of the merchant and innkeeper we are reminded that the Magician must also be grounded in the consciousness of the material world. He must walk between the two worlds of mind and matter in true balance.

In the Cary-Yale Visconti deck, dating from fifteenth-century Italy, we find the first depiction of the Magician with the four classic ritual tools of Western Occultism (opposite): the pentacle, blade, chalice, and wand. In his left hand he holds the wand upward as his right hand points down to the pentacle. This gesture is the classic posture of invocation, the calling down of the higher nature to the lower nature. It symbolizes the occult principle of "as above, so below" in which the Magician is the connecting bridge between the two planes.

The Magician is also a mystical warrior involved in the battle of the forces of Light and Darkness. The tools the Magician uses are reflections of the weapons that a knight carries into battle. The pentacle is the shield, the wand is the lance, the blade is the sword, and the chalice is the helmet. In a metaphysical sense we say that the pentacle is the shield of valor, the courage of one's own convictions. The wand is the extension of intuition. The blade is the cutting edge of reason, and the chalice is the accumulation of compassion. To walk the path of magick the Wiccan must be ethical, intuitive, strong willed, and compassionate to those whom he or she encounters on the Path.

The pentacle is a tool representing the Physical Plane as well as the Element of Earth. It is the shield of the magickal knight in his or her quest for knowledge. The pentacle serves to keep the magician grounded in the reality of the physical dimension in which he or she is currently operating. In this respect it is a symbolic reminder of reason and practicality.

The Magician

The Magician card from the Cary-Yale Visconti Tarocchi deck reproduced by permission of U.S. Games Systems, Inc., Stamford, CT 06902 USA, Copyright ©1985 by U.S. Games Systems, Inc. Further reproduction prohibited.

The wand is a tool representing the spiritual dimension as well as the Element of air. It is the lance of the knight, symbolic of his or her allegiance to a higher power. The blade represents the realm of the Mental Plane as it pertains to the will. It also represents the element of fire. The blade serves to banish illusion and delusion. It severs connections and directs energy as a raw force. The chalice is a tool representing the Divine Plane as well as the element of water. Water is associated with the moon, which in turn connects it to the astral material. Water takes on the shape of the chalice just as the astral material takes on the shape of the thought-form.

Symbolism of the Rider Tarot Magician

The symbolism contained in the Tarot reveals a great deal concerning the nature of the Magician. The Rider Tarot deck is a good one to focus on because it was printed prior to the individual adaptations made to Tarot decks during the late 1970s and early 1980s. Therefore it still contains much of the hidden symbolism that was overlooked in later versions. Above all, the Magician is a card of transformation. It is the first character encountered by the Fool in his or her journey through the Major Arcana. The Magician transforms the Fool so that he may be prepared to approach the High Priestess in the following card.

The Magician is standing beneath an arbor of roses. Roses represent desire; because of their relationship to Venus they specifically symbolize desires of the heart. The roses tell us that the powers the Magician draws from on high are modified by his or her personal passion or desire. Therefore we can discern the Magician's consciousness by those things which he or she brings into his or her life.

Hovering just over the Magician's head is the symbol for eternity. It is also the number eight resting on its side and is symbolic of Hermes or Mercury, the god of communication. This tells us that the Magician is connected to the momentum of the past, to the Akashic Records, to all that has been. He or she stands in the current of Time. The Magician's dark hair represents ignorance stemming from the human condition. The headband symbolizes a limit to this ignorance achieved by the knowledge accumulated by the Magician.

The Magician holds a wand raised in the right hand, while the left hand points down to the Earth. This symbolizes the higher nature invoked into the lower nature. This is the acquisition of true will I spoke of earlier. It is also a reflection of the principle "as above, so below." The wand is a phallic symbol symbolizing generative energy, the procreative force. Its base animal nature has been purified for spiritual purposes (sex magick) and this is reflected in the fact that the wand is colored white.

White is also the color of the Magician's robe and is symbolic of inner purification. Around the robe is a serpent biting its own tail, and thus serving as a belt around the robe of the Magician. The serpent represents wisdom and the Ob and Odic forces addressed in chapter seven. Thus the purified inner nature of the Magician is the equilibrium encircled by the serpent power. The red outer cloak is symbolic of desire and passion, even of the animal nature. It is depicted without a belt, symbolizing that the Magician is not bound by his or her passions and desires, and can wear or remove them as he or she pleases. This is both the gift and the burden of free will.

The Magician stands before the four classic ritual tools of Western Occultism. These represent the Four Elements of Creation. The Magician becomes the *Fifth Element* of Spirit overseeing the creative forces of the Elements. They also represent the Four Worlds of Occultism: Physical, Mental, Spiritual and Divine. In an occult sense these tools also represent the four admonitions of the Magician: to Know (chalice), to Will (blade), to Dare (wand), to be Silent (pentacle).

The final Tarot symbolism lies at the feet of the Magician. Here is depicted a beautiful garden of roses and lilies. The roses are wild roses, which have five petals. They represent desire as reflected by the five physical senses: taste, touch, sight, hearing, and smell. Lilies have six petals, the symbolic number of the Macrocosm. There are four lilies, representing the Four Worlds that comprise the Totality. The garden itself, at the feet of the Magician, represents the subconscious mind as well as self-consciousness. The symbols of desire here are a metaphor for the subconscious response to self-conscious direction. Desire is the catalyst to manifestation and yet it must be suppressed during the magickal act and be transformed into subconscious imagery. This is one of the keys to magick. It is also the principle of sigil magick.

The Magician card teaches us that personal power originates from conscious control of the forces and things that lie within the subconscious and self-conscious levels. The posture of the Magician illustrates that the energy comes to us from above. It is drawn, modified by acts of attention, and then directed by the will of the Magician. The Magician becomes the channel through which the forces of a higher nature flow into the Physical Plane. The balance for the Magician is to know that he or she is no longer the Fool, but also to know that he or she is not yet equal to that consciousness which we call the High Priestess.

The Code of Ethics

In Wicca the code of ethics or personal conduct is summed up in the words of the Wiccan Rede, which says that our actions should not intentionally harm another. The path of magick in Wicca teaches personal power and personal empowerment. It also teaches personal responsibility and reveals that everything is connected together. It is like a web, the threads of which are joined together. Any vibration causes a reaction felt by every other thread. It is from this law of *cause and effect, action and reaction,* that the code of ethics for Wiccans arises.

A Wiccan lives by a code of ethics that is built on the Laws of Nature. Behavior is not regulated by a fear of what awaits one in the afterlife but a respect for what awaits one in this life.

Everything and everyone is connected. What we do to one another, and to our world, we do to ourselves. In Wicca this is the foundation for the intent of the Rede:

Eight words the Wiccan Rede fulfills; if it harms none, do what you will.

Every act performed will draw to itself three times the nature of the act. In other words, affecting us mentality, spiritually, and physically. Some Wiccans believe that the energy we put out comes back three times as strong (the so-called Three-Fold Law of Return.). However, since there is no counterpart to this concept in Nature (and within Nature is the reflection of the Creators) this interpretation of the three-fold law is not embraced within the old initiate level teachings. The Craft is a Nature religion, and the old initiate levels always look at Nature as the blueprint for theology and magickal structure.

The Three-Fold Law affects not only our daily actions but also impacts the future as well. Here the law establishes those debts which must be paid. We call this the Threefold Law. This affects not only our daily actions but also impacts the future as well. We call this principle Karma. Therefore it is wise to always consider one's actions. Nothing escapes the Law of Karma and nothing is hidden from it. The law does not punish or reward. It only returns the intent of each action to its source of origin. By analogy, if you step off a cliff you will fall. There is no intent on either the part of the cliff or gravity. There is nothing good or evil about falling. The nature of the descent itself is only a law or a principle. So too is the nature of the Law of Three-fold return.

As noted, the Wiccan Rede says *"and as it harm none, do as thou wilt."* It is easy to interpret this to mean "do whatever you want as long as you don't harm anyone in the meantime." The inner teachings actually state that each person must seek out their True Will, the nature of their Higher Self. By doing so one is attuned to the *Spiritual Plan* which has been established for them (or by them, depending upon your view). Once you are attuned to your Higher Nature, no one can be harmed by your actions because you are following a spiritual plan of which they themselves are also a part. This is the understanding of the connectivity of all things and of the Law of Three-Fold return. We were not meant to simply wander about doing whatever feels right, without regard to a goal and the impact of that goal. We have a responsibility to ourselves and to each other.

The Eight-Fold Path

The Eight-Fold Path represents the traditional eight aspects of magickal and religious training which must be mastered in order to become an Adept or Master/Magus of the Arts:

1. Mental discipline through fasting and physical disciplines.

2. Development of the Will through mental imagery, visualization, and meditation.

3. Proper controlled use of drugs (hemp, peyote, mescaline, alcohol).

4. Personal power, thought-projection, raising and drawing power.

5. The Keys: ritual knowledge and practice. Use of enchantments, spells, symbols, and charms.

6. Psychic development and dream control.

7. Rising upon the Planes. Astral projection and mental projection.

8. Sex Magic, sensuality, and eroticism.

Mental discipline is an important aspect of magickal training. It strengthens the will and sharpens the mind. When a person possesses self-discipline and a strong will, then the Wiccan phrase "as my will/word, so mote it be!" takes on powerful meaning. Today many people employ such things as yoga and dieting in order to learn self-discipline. Once discipline is achieved, then the will can be further strengthened by the practice of visualization and meditation. A good method to begin with is to simply think of an object—an airplane, for example. Once you have it in your mind, begin to detail your image. Which way is the plane facing? What color is it, how big is it? Look further into its design, its curves, and think about its texture. This will help you develop a strong mind for visualizing astral images.

The use of drugs and alcohol is a very controversial subject. Certainly in ancient times alkaloid plants were used, along with ergot mold, to induce trance and altered states of consciousness. In Wicca today we still find the presence of wine, which was itself an intoxicant in the ancient Mystery Cult of Dionysus. The cakes themselves once contained herbal ingredients designed to drug the coven members for the purposes of astral projection (flying to the Sabbat). Like most things in Wicca today, the individual must decide for him- or herself what is appropriate and what is not.

Personal power, the ability to draw and raise energy, is an integral part of Wiccan magick. It is attained through several methods. Traditionally it was believed that by participating in each Sabbat of the year, and by observing each full moon ritual of the month, certain powers could be developed. This is because an individual is aligned and charged by the flow of energy concentrated in a ritual circle at such occasions as an Equinox or Solstice. Through such acts as practicing to raise a cone of power, and casting a circle by passing energy through one's blade, a Wiccan can become proficient at working with energy fields.

Learning the various correspondences employed in magick is important to the art. A knowledge of various herbs, enchantments, charms and spells helps to fine-tune the Wiccan's ability to direct energy. A working knowledge of how and why rituals function helps the Wiccan to focus and to draw upon the momentum of concepts still flowing from out of the past.

Like anything in life, practice is required in order to become skillful. You can only be as skilled as the time and energy you invest in the art of magick.

Psychic development is a very useful tool for the magician. It helps one to discern things of a nonphysical nature. This is important because if a person practices magick he or she is eventually going to encounter nonphysical entities. The psychic senses can help to perceive both the presence and the actions of various spirits and Elemental creatures. Breathing camphor fumes and drinking rosemary tea when the moon is full will aid in the development of psychic abilities. Dream control is another method that can be employed to train the psychic mind. (See appendix four for further information.)

Astral projection and rising on the planes are aspects of Wiccan practice designed to allow the Wiccan to access nonphysical realms and states of consciousness. In the ancient Mystery Cults it was used to negate the fear of death by proving to the initiate that he or she could still exist outside of the flesh. The projection of the astral body is something that everyone does while they sleep. It is the dream body that we see in dreams and its senses are what allow us to see and to feel while in the dream state. Conscious projection of the mind into the astral body is the goal. In this way we can operate in a conscious manner while exploring astral dimensions. See appendix three for projection techniques.

The use of sex magick in Wicca is perhaps an even more controversial subject than the use of drugs and alcohol. The Paganism from which Wicca evolved was essentially that of a fertility religion. Sexuality and sensuality were part of traditional Pagan rites intended to ensure a bountiful harvest or a successful hunt. In modern Wicca many practitioners employ symbolic acts that mimic sexual union. Thus it is common in Wiccan circles to insert the wand or blade into the chalice, replacing what was once a rite of sexual union. Sexual energy was once the battery that empowered the old rites. It typically followed erotic dancing and provocative chants.

These eight traditional aspects of magickal/religious train-ing within Wicca can be found in shamanistic traditions throughout the world, as well as in the mystical disciplines of Eastern practices. Tantric Yoga is a good example of the East-ern practice wherein the Kundalini force is evoked. The Eight-Fold path is a guideline to those who are interested in what the ancients believed to be the necessary steps to personal power. A personal study of each of these aspects will provide the magician with the tools through which deeper levels of mag-ickal knowledge can be obtained.

The Forces of Light and Darkness

The teachings of the Old Ways speak of primal powers known as the Forces of Light and Darkness. Throughout the ages Myths have depicted various gods and spirits engaged in the battle of good against evil. In this we see the timeless struggle for equilibrium between the forces that comprise Duality, the endless ebb and flow of the forces of Ob and Od. We see this reflected in the myths of the warring gods of Asgard, the Olympian gods and the Titans, and the battles of the Tuatha de Danan.

On a personal level we encounter these forces in the events of our own lives. Our lives are a combination of advances and setbacks, gains and losses, pleasures and pains. In the first degree initiation ceremony the initiate is told that suffering leads to the attainment of wisdom and compassion. In this manner we come to know that pain, despair, and all the obsta-cles we sometimes find in life are actually blessings of Dark-ness. Pain and despair teach us compassion. Obstacles teach us patience and endurance. They strengthen us so that we may walk the Path. Without these things we cannot grow in wis-dom as spiritual beings.

The blessings of Light are love, fellowship, success, and plea-sure. They teach us of the higher nature, or what some may call the divine nature. As spiritual beings encased in physical forms we require the nourishment of the blessings of Light in order to thrive, but Light has no meaning without Darkness, for one defines the other. Pain gives pleasure its value, just as defeat gives success its sweetness. In the reverse, pain would lose its power if pleasure was a thing unknown. Defeat would lose its sting if success did not exist. Light and Darkness are essential to an understanding of one another.

In Nature we see the duality of Light and Darkness reflected in the struggle for survival and in the cycles of the seasons. The waxing and waning powers of Nature are personified in such mythic figures as the Holly King and the Oak King of northern Europe. In southern Europe we find the Stag and Wolf gods symbolizing these forces. These kings and gods are the personification of the forces of Light and Darkness, the endless cycles of growth and decay. The Magician accepts and embraces these forces in his or her life. They are nourishment for the inner spirit, and in them the Magician chooses to discern the blessings of Light and Darkness.

The Magician lives outside of the forces of random occurrence. The teachings of the Old Ways tell us that when we celebrate the Wheel of the Year and observe each full moon we become part of *the way of things*. Therefore random occurrence is no longer woven into the patterns of our lives. Instead our lives become a tapestry of the patterns of Light and Darkness. The Magician sees life as an endless bestowing of blessings from the cycles of Duality. He or she becomes the conscious middle pillar, the equilibrium around which coil the serpents of Ob and Od. In a true sense the Magician becomes self-directed, the captain of his or her own soul. This is why it is imperative that the Magician take up the quest for his or her true will or higher nature. In Wicca the Magician works within the religious framework. From union with the God and Goddess, and by rapport with the Watchers, he or she is assisted and truly never walks alone. This is truly the walk of balance on the Magickal Path, flanked by the twin serpents of Od and Ob.

Appendices

We find the ancient continually confirming the extreme antiquity of the modern. Be it a tract here, a small observance there, now an herb in an incantation, and anon a couplet in a charm, they continually interlace, cross, touch, and coincide. I find these unobserved small identities continually manifesting themselves, and they form a chain of intrinsic evidence which is as valuable to a truly critical scholar as any historical or directly traditional confirmation.

—Charles Leland

Appendix One

Symbolic Natures

This section presents a list of natural and supernatural objects, as well as mystical themes, that all have a place in Wiccan beliefs and practices. In most cases the symbolism here is pre-Christian, although as the reader will see, much of this symbolism appears in Christianity as well. It is my desire, however, to make available here ancient pre-Christian European symbology. Though not an exhaustive list, I believe that the following will prove to be a valuable source of research for those wishing to further enhance or empower their own Traditions, rituals, and works of magick.

AIR: One of the four metaphysical Elements. It is considered *active* and *male* in nature. Air is the substance employed by things of the spirit, such as Sylphs and Fairies.

ANTS: Insects sacred to Ceres, and used in divination, whereby their movements were considered to have occult significance.

ANVIL: An Earth symbol and therefore symbolic of receptive energy. The hammer, a male symbol, when used in connection with the anvil symbolizes the mystical act of creation. See Hammer Gods.

APPLE: An ancient symbol of Totality. In later times it has come to also symbolize desire and indulgence. An apple sliced in half vertically has the appearance of female genitalia, and if sliced horizontally a pentagram is apparent. In Greek mythology Dionysus created the apple and gave it to Aphrodite as a symbol of love. The goddess Gaea presented Hera with an apple as a wish for fertility in her marriage to Zeus. In Celtic lore the apple symbolized ancestral knowledge. In the cult of the Norse goddess Iduna the apple symbolized eternal youth.

ASHES: A symbol of transition. They are also used to mark periods of passage. In the Mediterranean ashes are a symbol of death and purification. In a metaphysical sense ashes contain the essence of the power of that which was burned. Therefore ashes can be used in magickal works intended to anoint, connect or bind.

AUTUMN EQUINOX: The time of the Descent of the Goddess into the Underworld. With Her departure we see the decline of Nature and the coming of Winter. This is a classic ancient Mythos seen in the Sumerian myth of Inanna and in the ancient Greek and Roman legends of Demeter and Persephone. At this Equinox we also bid farewell to the Harvest Lord who was slain at Lammas (see Harvest Lord). The Eleusinian Mysteries, originating in Greece, involve themes of descent and ascent, loss and regain, light and darkness, and the cycles of life and death. Rites associated with these Mysteries were performed at midnight during the Spring and Autumn Equinoxes.

The Eleusinian Mysteries dealt with the abduction of Persephone by the Underworld God, a classic descent myth, and with the Quest for the return of the Goddess. Such rites were performed in honor of Ceres, an Agricultural Goddess who was Patron of the Mysteries. In the general mythos Persephone descends into the Underworld and encounters its Lord. Thus Life disappears with Her and the first autumn/winter befalls the Earth. The Lord of the Underworld falls in love with Persephone and wants to keep Her in His realm. The gods intervene, pleading with the Underworld Lord to release Persephone. First He refuses because Persephone has eaten the seeds of the pomegranate, an ancient symbol of the male seed (as noted in the Wiccan Descent Legend *they loved and were One*). Eventually He agrees on the condition that She return again to His realm for half of each year.

AXE: Symbolic of the power of Light. In ancient Greece it was the symbol of thunder and fire, due to its tendency to produce sparks in battle. As one of the earliest formal tools used in sacrificial rites it became a symbol of blood sacrifice, and later a symbol of royal blood. This resulted in it also becoming a symbol of royalty and authority connected to the Slain God or Harvest Lord mythos. The symbol of ancient Rome's power was the fasces, which was an axe bound in a bundle of harvested reeds.

AXE, DOUBLE-HEADED: In ancient Minoan Crete the double-bladed axe was a lunar symbol containing the waning and waxing crescents. The double-bladed axe, or labrys, also symbolizes the sacrificial king who stands between Earth and the Otherworld. It is often displayed with the head of a bull, which itself is a symbol of Dionysus, one of the slain gods of ancient Greece. The axe became associated with the labyrinth due to its/connection with bull gods and specifically with the minotaur.

AS ABOVE, SO BELOW: This phrase addresses the metaphysical concept that each Dimension is a lesser reflection of the one above it. The origin of this teaching is said to have come from the legendary Hermes Trismegistus, an Egyptian philosopher. In 1871 Paschal B. Randolph published a copy of the *Divine Pymander,* which was a reprint of an earlier work by Dr. Everard published in 1650, where we read: *"that which is below is as that which is above, for performing the miracles of the One Thing; and as all things are from one, by the mediation of one, so all things arose from this one thing by adaptation; the father of it is the Sun, the mother of it is the Moon; the Wind carried it in its belly; the name thereof is the Earth."[1]*

BAT: A symbol of the power of night and darkness. In ancient Europe it was related to dragon symbolism because it was winged and lived in a cave. The bat is also a symbol of the death and the Underworld.

BAUBO: A Greek mythological figure consisting only of a face implanted upon the lower half of a female body (the vulva personified). In the Eleusinian Mysteries she was a maidservant who performed an obscene belly dance for the goddess Demeter in an attempt to take her mind off Persephone, who had been kidnapped by the Lord of the Underworld. Demeter laughed and transformed her into the Baubo figure from that day forward.

BEAR: A symbol of instincts and beginnings. Bears are shown with such goddesses as Athena, Artemis, and Artio. In dream analysis, bears are often viewed as the dangerous aspect of the unconscious. The berserkers wore bear skins into battle to empower themselves with the spirit of this animal.

BEE: A symbol of purity. In the Greek Mystery traditions the bee symbolized the soul. The harmony of the beehive was a spiritual symbol of the Community of Souls. See honey.

BELL: A symbol of the creative force. In the Mystery tradition bells are symbols of both invocation and banishment. Hung from a cord they symbolize the human soul suspended between heaven and Earth.

BIRD: A symbol of the soul and the divine in many mythologies. The earliest goddess images found in the Neolithic period are bird deities. In Fairy Tales birds are often mystical messengers and guides.

---

1   Rosicrucian Publishing Company, 1871.

BLACKSMITH: The Blacksmith has long been associated with magickal traditions and the secrets of transformation. The Blacksmith is the astral shaman manifesting material objects. In some myths he is the lame god, crippled in order to keep him from running away.

BLOOD: A symbol of the Life Force itself. Blood is also a symbol of passion and sexuality. In a magickal sense, blood represents union and linking in general. The Blood Mysteries are marked by Birth, Sex, and Death. Menstrual blood is considered magickal in lunar cults. The flow of blood, and its ceasing, are both intimately connected to the Women's Mysteries. Menstruation, pregnancy, childbirth, and menopause are all aspects of the life cycle of women. Blood, or its absence, naturally marks the transformational stages of a woman, from the breaking of the hymen, to the blood of childbirth, to the cessation of bleeding at menopause.

BOAR: A symbol of both intrepidness and licentiousness, it was a sacred animal of the Celts and symbolized courage and strength.

BONES: A symbol of both death and resurrection. Just as seeds were buried in the Earth for a new harvest, bones were buried to "re-seed" the individual. In Witchcraft the skull and crossbones represent the Lord of the Underworld. In ancient times the skull of the last Harvest Lord was kept for ritual use until the next harvest.

BOW: A symbol of the power that issues forth from the light rays of the sun and moon.

BROOM: Witches' brooms were traditionally made from an ash handle, a birch twig for the brush, and Willow for the binding string, in honor of Hecate. The stick, brush, and cord are symbolic of Triformis. In herbal lore, ash protects from storms and drowning, birch binds evil spirits, and willow is sacred to Hecate. Thus the broom itself is a Triformis symbol.

BULL: A symbol of fertility, death, and resurrection. The bull was sacred to the Egyptians, Greeks, and Celts. In Egypt the god Osiris was associated with the bull, as was Dionysus in Greece.

BUTTERFLY: A symbol of the soul in many cultures. Also a symbol of metamorphosis and rebirth.

CADUCEUS: A symbol of harmony, peace, and reconciliation. In the Greek and Roman Mystery Cults the caduceus also represented the four elements: Earth (wand), Air (winged orb), Fire, and Water (the serpents and their undulating motions suggesting waves and their darting tongues suggesting flames). In a magickal sense it represents the equilibrium of opposing forces.

CAULDRON: A symbol of transmutation, germination, and transformation. It is also a womb symbol and therefore a goddess symbol as well. In Celtic lore it is often located in the Underworld or beneath a body of water (see water). In Greek and Roman myths it is often hidden in a cave (see cave).

CAVE: A symbol of things hidden or unrevealed. In Greek and Roman mythology it is often a doorway to the Underworld. Caves are also meeting places and places of birth for deities. In Neolithic times caves were dark womb symbols of the Great Goddess.

CENTAURS: In mythology, creatures half human and half horse. According to some sources, when horseback warriors from Asia first appeared to the matrifocal inhabitants of the Mediterranean, they were thought to be one creature. In Greek mythology the Centaurs were enemies of the Amazons and so there may be some historical basis for these myths. Originally the Centaur was a symbol of discord and internal disharmony. In classical mythology the Centaur became a mentor figure, a healer, and a teacher.

CHALICE: A symbol of containment. The opening represents receptivity to spiritual energy. The base is symbolic of the material world and the stem represents the connection between heaven and Earth.

CHILD OF PROMISE: A complex theme marking the further evolution of human understanding concerning the secrets of Nature. The Child is essentially two different principles, the son (and lover-to-be) of the Goddess and also the product of magick (meaning that it is what results from a work of magick). He appears in both the religion of Old Europe and in the Mystery Teachings of Witchcraft and Wicca.

CIRCLE: A symbol of ever-repeating cycles and of eternity. From the Earth, the sun and the moon appear like circles and this no doubt made an impression on the human psyche. To be inside a circle was to be inside the sacred sphere of the Sun God and Moon Goddess.

CONE OF POWER: An energy sphere raised by Wiccans in a ritual circle. Its purpose is to send energy for healing, spell casting, and other works of magick.

CORN BABY: The newborn spirit of the corn given birth in the harvest field. The Corn Baby is the symbol of new life appearing from old. Thus life continues in an unending cycle.

CORN MOTHER: The indwelling spirit of the ripe grain which gives life to the next year's crops. The wind passing through the crops is her spirit.

CORN SPIRIT: The embodiment in vegetable form of the animating spirit of the crops. In most cases the corn spirit is represented by the last sheaf, known as the Kern or Corn Baby.

CORNUCOPIA: A symbol of the fruits of one's labor. A harvest symbol.

CRESCENT: A symbol of the waxing or waning power of the moon. A symbol of beginnings.

CROSSROADS: A symbol of union, and in Jungian imagery a symbol of the Mother (the epitome and object of all union). In the Aegean/Mediterranean area, crossroads were sacred to Hecate Triformis.

CROW: In many mythologies the crow is a creator of the visible and invisible worlds. Crows are birds of omen and prophecy just as is the raven. To the Greeks and Romans the crow was associated with the god Saturn or Chronus. Among the Celts it was associated with the god Bran. Crows are said to have the power of divination and their "caws" are often considered warnings or directives.

CYPRESS: A symbol of the Lord of the Underworld. This is a very common tree to see growing in a cemetery. The cypress tree is also associated with the Watchers or Grigori (see Watchers).

DARKNESS: The forces of decline and opposition. Through them we learn and grow as spiritual beings, for without a knowledge of pain there can be no compassion.

DEW: In ancient times this was considered to be a fertile substance left by Eos, the Goddess of the Dawn. The goddess Diana was known as The Dewy One. In the dry warm climate of southern Europe the dew was essential for plant life. The life-giving and fertile quality of liquids under the power of the Goddess is apparent in an ancient fertility rite from southern Europe: A woman who wishes to become pregnant would lie nude on her back, beneath the full moon until sunrise. Thus was she covered with a bath of dew, considered to be a powerful potion for fertility.

DRAGON: In Western Occultism there are two types of Dragons: the *Terrestrial Dragon* and the *Celestial Dragon*. The Terrestrial Dragon represents the forces of *Darkness* and the Celestial Dragon represents the forces of *Light*. In European legends the Dragon who must be slain is the Terrestrial Dragon, representing the bestial nature which binds men and women to the material plane of existence. Traditionally a treasure is obtained or a prize won when the Dragon is slain. This is symbolic of spiritual liberation or enlightenment.

DUALITY: An occult principle stating that everything exists along with its opposite. The one nature defines the other as in good and evil, light and dark, positive and negative, male and female, etc.

EAST: The quarter associated with the Element of Air. In its connection to the rising of the sun and moon, the East is known as the portal of beginnings and the direction of enlightenment.

EGG: The Source of Life and the concealment of Mystery. In the Greek Orphic tradition the World itself was born of an egg laid by the Goddess of Night who was impregnated by the God of Wind. Eggs are also symbols of rebirth and regeneration.

EGREGORE: See glossary.

ELEMENTS: See glossary.

FAIRIES: Spiritual beings whose actions maintain the life force in Nature. The Fairy concept dates back to the Neolithic Cult of the Dead in Old Europe and to the ancient burial mounds.

FATES: The three goddesses of Fate or Destiny, also symbolizing the maiden, mother, and crone aspects of the Triformis nature of the Goddess. In their myths they spin the pattern of human life and then cut the final thread which initiates the death of an individual. In Germanic lore the Fates were known as the Norns (the Wyrrd Sisters). The Germanics gave them the names Urd, Verdandi and Skuld (also known as Wyrd, Werthende, and Should). In the earlier Greek tradition they were called Klotho, Lachesis, and Atropos. In both cultures the three sisters spun the thread of life and then cut it, bringing a person's time on the Earth to an end. Among the Greeks, Klotho (the youngest) put the wool around the spindle. Lachesis (the middle sister) spun it and Atropos (the Eldest) cut if off. In Germanic lore Skuld (the youngest) cut the thread, while Urd (the Eldest) wrapped the wool and Verdandi (the middle sister) spun it.

FIRE: Sometimes known as the living Element, Fire is an ancient symbol of divinity. It is also the living principle of Duality, providing light and heat to aid humankind while at the same time being a force of death and destruction. The eternal flame is a common theme in ancient Mystery Cults and typically represents the eternal presence of divinity.

FISH: Because of their connection with water, fish are symbols of fertility. In ancient times fish were called birds of the Underworld because of their movement beneath the water. From this Other World nature they came to be associated with the subconscious mind and with psychic abilities. We see this in the Zodiac sign of Pisces the fish. See water.

FISHER KING: A character belonging to the Grail mythos in which he is the monarch in a mythical castle. Here he is seen as the *Fisher of Men,* which is an aspect of mystical Christianity. To fish is to extract and in a mystical sense the water is the depths of one's own inner being. The fish is the consciousness moving in the depths of one's soul. The Fisher King catches a fish that feeds the entire company of people in his vicinity. In the mythos the King is the fisher of men with the ability to bring forth the souls of others from the hidden depths of the innerself.

FLOGGING: In ancient Mystery Cults an act of purification. Flogging was believed to drive out evil spirits and to sharpen the senses. In this sense flogging was an act of regeneration.

FOOL: In the Tarot the Fool is the seeker who sets out upon the path of enlightenment without any prior knowledge of that which he seeks. He relies entirely on his own instincts and intuition. In the symbolism of the Tarot card the Fool is walking toward the edge of a cliff, unaware of the direction in which he is headed. He is totally absorbed in the Self, while the dog of reason barks unnoticed at his heels. The Fool is the sacrificial victim in European ritual themes, seen as one who willingly but unknowingly comes to his own demise. He is the sacrifice of the scapegoat. In him we see the Jester who reminds us of our own folly.

FROG: Frogs and toads have long been associated with Witch-craft. Frogs are symbols of fertility and transformation as reflected in the tadpole stage. Frogs were associated with rain and with the moon, both of which they were believed to have power over. Their rhythmical croaking was used by ancient Witches in the same manner as shamans use rhythmical drumming to induce trance.

GARGOYLES: A creature of the Mystery Cult tradition associated with guardianship. In order to weed out the unworthy, the ancient Sages created grotesque figures and formulas to symbolize various aspects of their teachings. If appearance alone was enough to turn someone away, then they were considered to be untrainable, so the gargoyle figure stood guard over the mysteries and is often seen above doorways or in supporting columns.

GARLAND: A symbol of the inner connections between all things. The garland is a symbol of that which binds and connects. Garlands are typically made from plants and flowers that symbolize the season or event for which the garland is hung as a marker or indicator.

GOAT: The female goat is a symbol of nurturing while the male goat is a symbol of virility and sexuality. The Inquisition often accused Witches of copulating with goats or with the devil in the form of a goat. The god Pan is half human and half goat, symbolizing the two natures of the higher and lower Self.

GRAIL: A symbol of spiritual transformation and purification. By some accounts a symbol of salvation as well. In mystical Christianity it is said to be the chalice used by Jesus in the Last Supper with his disciples. The Grail most likely evolved from early mystical cauldron concepts that originated in the old lunar cults. It usurped both the cauldron and lunar symbolism and a solar chalice sought after by male knights.

GRAIN: A symbol of regeneration and resurrection—the symbolic connection between burial and the planting of a seed is obvious enough. The grain issues forth new life in the Spring, itself having fallen from the death of last season's crop. A shaft of wheat is the most common symbol and often appears on old tombstones.

GREAT MOTHER: A concept growing out of the Neolithic cult of the Great Goddess. The Great Mother is the womb of Nature, the Gateway to and from the Worlds. All goddesses are contained within her and both life and death are children of her womb.

GUARDIAN: Ancient shrines and groves had their guardians in the days of antiquity. The Guardian serves to prevent the unprepared from gaining access to things that could be dangerous in their hands. In one sense the Guardian is the conscious rational mind, standing watch over the sub-conscious mind. When we dismiss something we experienced as *just our imagination,* this is the Guardian cutting us off from the mystical connection. Only dedication and persistence can feat the Guardian.

HAMMER: A symbol of thunder and fire. The hammer was a symbol of power and served as an emblem or wand of authority (like a scepter) in the hands of the old Hammer gods.

HAMMER GODS: In the vast majority of cases Hammer gods are deities associated with Death and physical injury. Altars dedicated to Hammer gods depict images of human limbs and offerings have been found that appear to indicate that the Hammer god was called upon to either repair or to forge and shape new limbs (perhaps for use in the Afterlife). The Hammer Gods are often depicted in rustic attire symbolizing a woodland nature. Hammer symbols appear on altars with dedications to the Roman Forest god Silvanus for example. Hammer gods often appear with a hammer, pot, and wolf skin or pelt. The wearing of an animal skin proclaims the Hammer god as a wild deity of the woodlands.

In the Etruscan religion the Hammer god was known as Tuchulcha. He often appears standing in a doorway decorated with body parts around the frame. Tuchulcha was also a deity associated with Death and struck the dead person upon the head with his hammer. Such a blow removed the memory of life and awakened the person to the Underworld consciousness. The Celtic Hammer god was known as Sucellus. To the Romans he was Vulcan. In Nordic lore he was Thor.

HARVEST LORD: He is the Green Man seen as the Cycle of Nature in the plant kingdom. He is harvested and his seeds planted into the Earth so that life may continue and be ever more abundant. This mythos is symbolic of the planted seed nourished beneath the soil, and the ascending sprout that becomes the harvested plant by the time of the Autumn Equinox.

HAWK: In ancient times the hawk was a symbol of the freed soul.

HEARTH: A womb symbol and a symbol of Clan. The hearth was the focal point of Pagan life. Food was prepared there, family stories recounted there, and in many ancient cultures ancestral shrines were placed there. Spirits such as the Lare or Lasa were said to gather at the hearth. The Roman goddess Vesta was a deity connected with hearth and home.

HOLLY KING: A symbol of the waning forces of Nature. At the Winter Solstice he defeats his brother the Oak King in ritual combat and thus claims the Season. He is depicted as an old man in winter garb. His head bears a wreath of holly and he often carries a staff. Some Santa Claus figures are actually Holly King figures. See Oak King.

HONEY: In ancient times honey was used to anoint in initiation because the honey itself was the result of a mysterious process of transformation performed by bees. The gathering of honey from a beehive was a risky business in ancient times, and so honey also became the symbol of obtaining knowledge through pain. Honey was also used as an offering for the dead and thus we find the association of bees with departed souls.

HOODED ONE: One of the three aspects of the God in Wicca: the Hooded One, the Horned One, and the Old One. The Hooded One is the Green Man, hooded in the green of the forest. In later times he became the Harvest Lord, as humans left the forest for the fields.

HORAE: Ancient deities of the threefold seasons of Nature. Thallo represented blooming plants. Auxo symbolized growth and Carpo represented crops in their maturity. The word *Horae* is derived from the Greek word for time or hours. In essence the Horae are deities of agriculture and attend to the Harvest Lord.

HORNED ONE: The stag-horned god of the Old Religion. We also see him in various cultures as the bull-horned god and as the goat-horned god. He is a symbol of fertility, virility, and of all that is wild and undomesticated.

HORNS: Ancient symbols of power and virility. Horns are generally considered lunar symbols because they resemble crescent moons. The horns of stags, goats, and bulls were considered signs of fertility because these animals belonged to herds.

HORSE: A symbol of power and vitality. The stallion is also a symbol of virility. The imprint of a horse's hoofprint was a sign of its power, and to possess a horseshoe was a good luck symbol meaning that you were under its protection.

IRON: A metal used in counter-magick. Items made of iron such as horseshoes and religious symbols were all used to banish evil. Iron is a readily magnetized metal that can absorb and retain magnetic charges quite easily. Because of this nature it was believed to rob nearby objects of whatever magick they might contain.

IVY: A symbol of true love and friendship due to its nature of clinging to anything it encounters with great tenacity. The ancients believed that ivy could control intoxication and is commonly worn by satyrs and other followers of Dionysus as depicted in ancient art. The Thyrsus carried by Dionysus was entwined with both vine leaves and ivy. The ivy was the balance to the grapevine and thus provided equilibrium to Dinoysus himself.

KNOT: Knots represent many things: tying, untying, release, retention, unity, binding, confining, and confirming. They are used in Folk Magick to bind or fix a spell.

LABYRINTH: A symbol of the path of Initiation and enlightenment. Ancient historians mention the presence of the labyrinth in Egypt (Lake Moeris), Greece (Lemnos), Crete (Cnossus), and Etrusca (Clusium). Generally speaking, the maze was a system of complex pathways. Once inside, it was difficult if not impossible to find one's way back out.

LADY OF THE LAKE: Originally guardian spirits of sacred lakes and other bodies of water. Water is essentially a feminine element and thus spirits of the water are quite often female in Nature. With the passage of time the concept of female deity who guarded and empowered such sacred sites arose. In northern Europe the Lady of the Lake is connected to the King Arthur legends surrounding the magickal sword Excalibur. In southern Europe the Lady of the Lake is Egeria, a water nymph at the sanctuary of Diana at Lake Nemi (the lake itself is called *Diana's Mirror*). The Guardian of the grove at Nemi was known as *Rex Nemorensis* (the King of the Woods) and he bore a sword. His relationship to Egeria was not unlike that of Arthur and the Lady of the Lake from whom he received Excalibur.

MENHIR: A rough-hewn standing stone of the Neolithic period whose purpose is still open to debate. Some people believe they guard burial sites, mark out astronomical sites, house powerful spirits, or indicate the location of portals to other dimensions.

MISTLETOE: A symbol of immortality and love. Mistletoe growing on oak trees was highly regarded by the Romans and the Celts as a sacred plant. Because the juice of its berries resembles semen it was thought to be the sperm of the Oak Tree God and was therefore considered to be of great power.

MUSES: The symbol of inspiration. The Muses were the daughters of Zeus and the nymph Mnemosyne who inspired the arts. They were Clio (history), Melpomene (tragedy), Terpsichore (poetry and dance), Thalia (comedy), Euterpe (flute), Erato (love poetry), Urania (astronomy), Polyhymnia (heroic hymns and mimicry), and Calliope (epic poetry).

NORTH: Since ancient times a place of great power. The Celts associate the north with many of their gods. The ancient Etruscans placed their highest god and goddess at the north. In Wicca the altar is set so that the coven members face north when they stand before it.

OAK KING: A symbol of the waxing powers of Nature. At the Summer Solstice he defeats his brother the Holly King in ritual combat and captures the Season. He is depicted as a woodsman wearing a wreath of oak leaves on his head. Often he is depicted with a tree and various forest animals beside him. Some Santa Claus figures are actually Oak Kings. See Holly King.

OLD ONE: A term for the Green Man as Lord of the Forest. This recalls his nature prior to the development of agriculture.

OLD ONES: A term for the primal spirits of Nature. This relates to their nature before humans personified them.

OWL: A symbol of both Death and Wisdom in European lore. Because of the spiral patterns noted on many owl feathers, especially around the eyes, owls were connected with the tombs of the Neolithic cult of the Dead which featured spiral designs. Owls appear with goddesses of wisdom in many cultures. In southern Europe the owl is sacred to Athena and in northern Europe it is sacred to Blodeuwedd.

POMEGRANATE: A sign of fertility. In Patriarchal lore it is symbolic of male semen and in Matriarchal lore it symbolizes the Women's Mysteries as they apply to the blood mysteries: birth, sex, and death. See Autumn Equinox.

RAVEN: A symbol of occult knowledge. In myth and legend a trickster spirit who sets people up in situations of adversity through which they learn many things. In Old Europe the raven was also a symbol of death and an omen of misfortune. In European myths the raven is often a messenger of the gods.

ROOSTER: In European lore the cock is associated with the sun god Apollo. In legend the rooster crows at dawn and awakens the sun, which banishes evil spirits. Thus the cock is a symbol of protection and banishment.

SALAMANDER: A spirit of the Element of Fire.

SERPENT: A symbol of Wisdom and Craftiness. Serpents also represent the animation of various principles and concepts such as the Kundalini force, the forces of Light and Darkness, and the power of the Od and the Ob.

SKULL: In the Mystery tradition a symbol of the inner nature stripped down to its foundation through the process of Initiation into the great Mysteries of Occultism. It is also a symbol of Death, whether dying in the flesh or the dying of Self/Ego.

SOUTH: In ancient occultism the quarter of astral forces. The south is the place of Elemental fire.

SPINDLE/SPINNING: Symbols of transformation and the magickal arts. Power symbols employed in the Women's Mystery Cult tradition.

SPIRAL: Neolithic symbols of death and trance. They are often seen depicted on ancient tombs. See Labyrinth.

SPRING EQUINOX: The celebration of the return of Spring. Among Wiccans it is a time to welcome the return of the Goddess from her sojourn into the Underworld. Beneath the soil long held in the embrace of Winter, the seeds of new life begin to awaken. In ancient times the first signs of budding trees announced the coming arrival of the Goddess. Ritual fires burned to encourage the sun to warm the soil and stir the sleeping life beneath it. Dancers came together upon the ancient sites to celebrate the Goddess and the promise of abundance symbolized by bud and leaf and stem.

The Vernal Equinox marks the first day of Spring. Modern Wiccans and Pagans associate the Goddess Ostara with this special Season. A form of this goddess name appears in such early Christian works as the *De Temporum Ratione* under the title Eostre (Ostre) who was the Anglo-Saxon goddess of Spring. In this text we find a connection between the German word *Ostern* denoting an Eastern orientation and the word "Easter." Thus the related goddess Ostre (Ostara) can be seen as a goddess of the East and therefore of the dawn. Modern Easter celebrations include a sunrise ceremony symbolic of the resurrection from death symbolized by the dawn. As the goddess of the East, Eostre was worshiped at this quarter of rebirth as the maiden aspect of Triformis, the Threefold Goddess.

STAG: A symbol of regeneration and rebirth. Also a symbol of the waxing year, the forces of Light. In ancient lore the stag was the enemy of serpents and its hide was worn as a protection against venom. In Celtic lore deer are said to be fairy cattle and the stag is seen as a messenger between the spirit world and the material world.

SUMMERLAND: In Wiccan theology the abode of the departed soul. It is likened to the Celtic realm of Tir Nan Og where the death journey is across the western waters. The Summerland is depicted as a Pagan paradise in which it is always Summer and everything is in abundance. The Summerland is populated by all the creatures of myth and legend. Here the departed soul rests and is renewed as it prepares for rebirth.

THRESHOLD: In occult terms an entryway into a temple or a ritual circle. In the Mystery Tradition the threshold is placed at the northeast point. This position represents the union of power with enlightenment. A threshold can also apply to an access point to states of consciousness.

TRIFORMIS: The threefold nature. In Wicca this is often viewed as the Maiden, Mother, and Crone aspect. In ancient times this was typified by the goddess Diana and by Hecate. We see it also in the Fates and the Horae of Aegean/Mediterranean religion. We later find this concept in Celtic lands after Roman occupation. The Celtic goddess Brighid is depicted as a threefold goddess, appearing very much like the Greek carvings of Hecate Triformis.

WATCHERS: In the Stellar Mythos the Watchers were gods who guarded the Heavens and the Earth. Their nature, as well as their "rank," was altered by the successive Lunar and Solar Cults which replaced the Stellar Cults. Eventually the Greeks reduced them to the Gods of the four winds, and the Christians to principalities of the air. Their connection with the Stars is vaguely recalled in the Christian concept of heavenly angels.

In the early Stellar Cults of Mesopotamia there were four "royal" Stars (known as Lords) which were called the Watchers. Each one of these Stars "ruled" over one of the four cardinal points common to astrology. This particular system would date from approximately 3000 B.C. The Star Aldebaran, when it marked the Vernal Equinox, held the position of Watcher of the East. Regulus, marking the Summer Solstice, was Watcher of the South. Antares, marking the Autumn Equinox, was Watcher of the West. Fomalhaut, marking the Winter Solstice, was Watcher of the North.

WATCHTOWERS: Towers were constructed bearing the symbols of the Watchers, as a form of worship, and their symbols were set upon the Towers for the purpose of evocation. These towers were called Ziggurats (cosmic mountains) and were said to have been 270 feet high. In part they served as primitive astronomical observatories, and were built with seven terraces representing the seven known planets of their era. During the "Rites of Calling" the Watcher's symbols were traced in the air using torches or ritual wands, and the secret names of the Watchers were called out.

WATER: Associated with the West quarter, it is one of the four Elements. Water is also a symbol of regeneration, renovation, and dissolution.

WELLS: Symbols of portals to the Underworld as well as to the realms of spirits and fairies. Wells were often sacred and magickal because of their association with spirits and deities.

WEST: The quarter associated with the element of Water. It is also the portal or gateway to the Underworld or the Summerland.

WHEEL OF THE YEAR: A term for the four seasons or cycles of Nature. It is often symbolized by an eight-spoke wheel, indicating each solstice and equinox as well as the days that fall exactly between them.

WINE: In Matrifocal times a symbol of the blood of the goddess, the life-giving essence. In Patriarchal times a symbol of the blood of the slain god. See Harvest Lord.

WOLF: A symbol of the waning period of Nature, of decline and death. The forces of Winter and of Darkness. See Stag.

Appendix Two

Tables of Correspondences

LUNAR CORRESPONDENCES

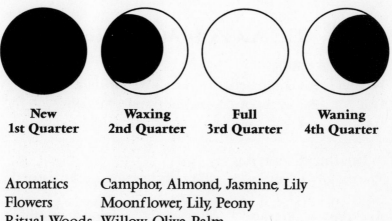

New	Waxing	Full	Waning
1st Quarter	2nd Quarter	3rd Quarter	4th Quarter

Aromatics   Camphor, Almond, Jasmine, Lily
Flowers   Moonflower, Lily, Peony
Ritual Woods   Willow, Olive, Palm
Number   9
Element   Water
Metal   Silver
Stone   Moonstone
Quarter   West

MOON NAMES

October	Hunter's Moon
November	Larder Moon
December	Long Night Moon
January	Winter Moon
February	Wolf Moon
March	Raven Moon
April	Meadow Moon
May	Goddess Moon
June	Rose Moon
July	Horn Moon
August	Piscary Moon
September	Harvest Moon

LUNAR ZODIAC FORCES

(When the Moon is)

Waxing	All constructive works, all beginnings
Full	All works of power and transformation
Waning	All works of dissolving or banishing

(When the Moon is in)

Taurus, Virgo, Capricorn	All works involving supernatural forces
Aries, Leo, Sagittarius	All works of love and friendship
Cancer, Scorpio, Pisces	All works involving crossing/hexes
Gemini, Libra, Aquarius	All works of an unusual nature

PLANETARY AROMATICS

Sun   Cinnamon
Moon   Almond, Jasmine, Camphor
Mercury   Cinquefoil, Fennel, Anise
Venus   Myrtle, Rose, Ambergris, Amber
Mars   Aloes, Dragon's Blood, Tobacco
Jupiter   Nutmeg, Juniper, Olive Oil
Saturn   Myrrh, Poppy, Asafoetida

SACRED TREES

Sun   Laurel and Oak
Moon   Willow, Olive, Palm
Mercury   Hickory
Venus   Hazel
Mars   Pine, Birch, Mulberry
Jupiter   Ash and Apple
Saturn   Elm

RITUAL COLOR SYMBOLISM

White   Purity, spiritual forces
Blue   Peace, spiritual knowledge
Green   Nature magick, love
Yellow   Vital force
Red   Life force, sexual energy
Brown   Neutralizing force
Black   Drawing, absorbing, receptivity, procreative

ELEMENTAL CORRESPONDENCES

EARTH	AIR	FIRE	WATER
North	East	South	West
Pentacle	Wand	Blade	Chalice
Gnomes	Sylphs	Salamanders	Undines
Winter	Spring	Summer	Fall
Land	Sky	Astral	Sea
Yellow	Blue	Red	Green
Parting	Friendship	Passion	Love
Terra	Cosmos	Sun	Moon
Strength	Intellect	Desire	Adaptivity
Patience	Persuasion	Force	Influence
Winter Solstice	Vernal Equinox	Summer Solstice	Autumn Equinox

RITUAL TOOL CORRESPONDENCES

PENTACLE	WAND	BLADE	CHALICE
Manifestation	Direction	Focus	Accumulation
Earth	Air	Fire	Water
Feminine	Masculine	Masculine	Feminine
North	East	South	West

NUMERICAL VALUE OF ALPHABET

A	B	C	D	E	F	G	H	I	J	K	L	M
1	2	3	4	5	8	3	5	1	1	2	3	4
N	O	P	Q	R	S	T	U	V	W	X	Y	Z
5	7	8	1	2	3	4	6	6	6	6	1	7

PLANETARY HOUR TABLE

After Sunrise	Sun	Mon	Tues	Wed	Thurs	Fri	Sat
1st	Sun	Moon	Mars	Mercury	Jupiter	Venus	Saturn
2nd	Venus	Saturn	Sun	Moon	Mars	Mercury	Jupiter
3rd	Mercury	Jupiter	Venus	Saturn	Sun	Moon	Mars
4th	Moon	Mars	Mercury	Jupiter	Venus	Saturn	Sun
5th	Saturn	Sun	Moon	Mars	Mercury	Jupiter	Venus
6th	Jupiter	Venus	Saturn	Sun	Moon	Mars	Mercury
7th	Mars	Mercury	Jupiter	Venus	Saturn	Sun	Moon
8th	Sun	Moon	Mars	Mercury	Jupiter	Venus	Saturn
9th	Venus	Saturn	Sun	Moon	Mars	Mercury	Jupiter
10th	Mercury	Jupiter	Venus	Saturn	Sun	Moon	Mars
11th	Moon	Mars	Mercury	Jupiter	Venus	Saturn	Sun
12th	Saturn	Sun	Moon	Mars	Mercury	Jupiter	Venus
13th	Jupiter	Venus	Saturn	Sun	Moon	Mars	Mercury
14th	Mars	Mercury	Jupiter	Venus	Saturn	Sun	Moon
15th	Sun	Moon	Mars	Mercury	Jupiter	Venus	Saturn
16th	Venus	Saturn	Sun	Moon	Mars	Mercury	Jupiter
17th	Mercury	Jupiter	Venus	Saturn	Sun	Moon	Mars
18th	Moon	Mars	Mercury	Jupiter	Venus	Saturn	Sun
19th	Saturn	Sun	Moon	Mars	Mercury	Jupiter	Venus
20th	Jupiter	Venus	Saturn	Sun	Moon	Mars	Mercury
21st	Mars	Mercury	Jupiter	Venus	Saturn	Sun	Moon
22nd	Sun	Moon	Mars	Mercury	Jupiter	Venus	Saturn
23rd	Venus	Saturn	Sun	Moon	Mars	Mercury	Jupiter
24th	Mercury	Jupiter	Venus	Saturn	Sun	Moon	Mars

MAGICKAL VALUES OF THE MOON

37	78	29	70	21	62	13	54	5
6	38	79	30	71	22	63	14	46
47	7	39	80	31	72	23	55	15
16	48	8	40	81	32	64	24	56
57	17	49	9	41	73	33	65	25
26	58	18	50	1	42	74	34	66
67	27	59	10	51	2	43	75	35
36	68	19	60	11	52	3	44	76
77	28	69	20	61	12	53	4	45

The purpose of this table is to draw out magickal sigils. Using the numerical alphabet in this appendix, write out the name of that which you wish to sigilize. Then assign a numerical value to each letter. Next place a piece of tracing paper over the Moon Table and circle the value of the first letter. Draw a line from there to the value of the next letter. Continue in an unbroken line until you reach the value of the last letter. Then mark it by simply crossing the line like the capital "T" letter. The resulting design is a sigil of what you desire.

Protective Pentagram with Spirit Symbols.

Appendix Three

Dream Working

Dream working is the use of dreams to gain access to subconscious levels of the mind. The tools required for this work are dream symbols and conscious control or alteration of the dream state. Dreams are the doorways to other realms of Consciousness. They are also portals to the Astral Plane. These realms are capable of bestowing knowledge and power to the discerning dreamer.

The first step in dream working is to understand your own inner symbolism. Some dream symbols are cultural in nature but the majority will be your own personal imagery. To begin, establish a dream diary recording each night's dreams. Mark the pages into sections with the following headings: Theme, Setting, People, Animals, Actions, Danger, Objects.

Immediately upon awakening, fill in the sections that apply. This will serve to save the memory of the dream. After completing this, write a detailed account of the dream using the headings to remind you of its contents. Do not dwell on aspects that tend to slip away. It is also a good idea to record the previous day's events on another piece of paper. This will serve to reveal any connection between a certain symbol and an actual event. If the symbol repeats when the action occurs, then you will have a clue to your inner symbolism.

Each month reflect back over the previous month's dreams. Look for symbols that seem to repeat and observe if they correspond to particular actions or situations that occurred within that month. Record any symbol and its meaning once you have established its pattern. Eventually you will have a private

"Dream Symbol Dictionary." Bear in mind, however, that these symbols may occur in different ways and the same symbol may appear differently in order to express an aspect of inner consciousness. If a symbol appears before an action occurs, and this seems to follow a pattern, then you may be experiencing dream divination. Keep track of daily actions and nightly dreams. Be sure to date each entry in your diary.

The second step in dream working is to establish conscious control of the dream. There are two simple methods of beginning this phase. First look back through your diary of symbols and see if any one setting has repeated itself more than three times. Look also for any person or situation that has also repeated its appearance in this manner, then proceed as follows:

The next time you encounter the person, setting, or situation (in the waking state) immediately look at your right hand. Affirm mentally that you have done this and that you are in control of every act that you perform. Repeat this on every occasion. This is important because you will be conditioning your subconscious mind for this response in the Dream World. Thus you will become conscious in the subconscious state the next time you encounter the person or situation in the dream state.

The second method is to repeat to yourself while falling asleep that you will look at your right hand while you are dreaming. Do this at least ten times per occasion. Whichever method you choose will probably require weeks in obtaining the goal. On the other hand, it may happen quickly. This differs with the individual. Once you have accomplished the goal of the exercise you will find yourself aware that you are dreaming. You will look at your right hand and thus become conscious in the dream state. This is because the conscious mind planted the suggestion and this becomes the magickal link between the conscious and subconscious minds.

Once you are aware that you are dreaming, you can then begin to experiment. Try changing the dream's setting or situation by thinking of something else. You can also choose to move to some area or person not intended in the theme of the dream. If you wish you may simply step outside of the dream and observe it as it continues. If this option arises you will know what I mean. Whatever you decide to do, have fun with it. Continue recording your dreams in the Dream Diary.

The final step now is to establish a *dream gate*. This is not a gate into the dream world but rather a gate to the *other side*. When working with the dream gate it is vital that you affirm to yourself that it is a doorway to an astral world. Care should always be taken to purify yourself and your environment when working with the dream gate. Sprinkle yourself with salted water and do the same to the objects around your work area (bedroom or whatever). Fume the area with an incense of Dragon's Blood. Advanced practitioners may choose to anoint themselves with charged oils and burn a lunar incense during the dream. Great care should always be taken when allowing incense to burn during sleep. A protective pentagram or special amulet may also be worn during the dream working to give you confidence on your journey.

To begin, you will need to draw an entry or exit that will symbolize the dream gate. Two of the most popular visualizations are the twin pillars or the curtain portal (see illustration, page 220). Once drawn, study the image and firmly impress it in your mind. Practice visualizing it in your mind several times each day. Visualize it as you drift off to sleep as this will help to connect it to the dream world. Tape the drawing to the ceiling above your bed if you so desire. Once you have established conscious control within the dream, begin looking for the dream gate. If you have properly impressed the image upon your mind, you will find it. Once you do, then pass through to the other side. It is essential that you return back through the gate once your experience is completed.

When entering through the portal of the pillars, the black one is on your left, the white on your right. When returning the order is *opposite*. Look at their positions on both sides each time that you pass through. If using the curtain, part it by putting both hands through it together (like diving into a swimming pool). The color of the curtain is purple. What awaits you on the other side is a separate reality attuned to all that is negative and positive within your own being.

Other Uses of the Pillars

The pillar image can also be used for meditation on a Tarot card, magickal image, or something with which you desire a mental, astral, or spiritual connection. The pillars will also serve nicely when employing the magickal caduceus design addressed in chapter seven. Place the Tarot card, caduceus, or other image in the center between the pillars. I suggest either putting the pillars on a poster board or in a picture frame so you can hang it on a wall. Once in place, you can mentally enter into the image. To do this, mentally see yourself projected into the Tarot card. Imagine moving about examining the images therein.

Using the techniques related to odic breath in chapters seven and eight, you can charge the pillar image and the symbol you placed. If you draw the image yourself, charge the pen/ink with odic breath. Liquids are better at holding a magickal charge for long periods than is paper. Another alternative is to place a drop of elemental condenser on each corner of the paper. This will help fix the charge to the paper. Elemental condensers are described in chapter five. You can also use the pillar design as a door way to your astral temple, as described in my book *The Wiccan Mysteries,* in appendix two.

Appendix Four

History of Western
Occultism

When we look at the moon today, we are gazing on the very same moon beneath which ancient Witches and sorcerers once gathered. The moon is not a symbol but an actual physical reminder of the mysterious forces linking us to our ancestors. These energies are the essence of magick. The story of magick and its survival into modern times is a fascinating testament to the tenacity of secret societies. Civilizations rose and fell over the centuries, dominated by various religions, yet magickal systems endured within the shadows of their subcultures. The Witch and the sorcerer, whether hunted or disbelieved, practiced their arts in secret over the passing centuries.

Magick as a system evolved out of primitive beliefs concerning both the *natural* and *supernatural* worlds. Caves, lakes, pits, and wells all portrayed entryways into the unseen worlds. Connections evolved from the offering of sacrifices in the physical world presented to the spiritual world. Sacred animals or objects were set within these holy places in exchange for the fruits of the Other World. In the early stages of this type of worship people believed in primal spirits. The image of a god or goddess appears newly expressed upon the walls of Paleolithic caves. By the Neolithic era we see divine images unquestionably related to religious beliefs and practices.

Before the appearance of temples in which to worship gods and goddesses, people met in sacred groves. The ancient people in both southern and northern Europe worshiped trees as divine beings. Veneration of the oak tree appears highly marked in ancient beliefs. The Druidic cult involved the worship of the oak. This is also true of the cult of Rex Nemorensis at the sanctuary of the goddess Diana AT Lake Nemi in Italy. The oak tree often appears as a symbol of the highest aspect of the deity.

Over many centuries objects associated with spirits and deities evolved into a framework of complex tables of correspondences Magickal knowledge involved understanding the connections and how to employ them in order to obtain the desired response. Various animal spirits could be enlisted to aid in a work of magick according to these various connections. The ancients viewed everything in Nature as alive and conscious, even down to the very rocks and stones themselves. To a certain extent, magickal abilities relate to rapport with a host of Nature spirits as reflected in these ancient associations.

Within each region of Europe a type of Paganism evolved, unique in many ways to the inhabitants of the region. The basic beliefs were quite similar, however, and there appears to have been an almost universal view of magick and the supernatural. Many changes occurred over the centuries due in large part to the Indo-European expansion into Old Europe, and the later conquests made by the Roman Empire. The Romans typically aligned the deities of conquered populations with their own to assimilate the newly acquired cultures. Romanized deities, along with Pagan and magickal concepts of the Mediterranean, replaced or modified the indigenous beliefs and practices of the conquered peoples throughout most of Europe.

With the collapse of the Roman Empire in the fifth century A.D., Europe fell into the Dark Ages. The Roman Catholic Church replaced Imperial Rome as the unifying factor in Europe. Latin remained the language of learned scholars and helped to preserve much of the knowledge we now possess about ancient cultures and about magick. Italy led Europe out of the Dark Ages with the Renaissance period beginning in the early fourteenth century. By the fifteenth century the Renaissance spread to France, Spain, England, and the Netherlands. Besides art, science, and literature, the Renaissance produced many books on natural magick and occult philosophy in general. Magick during this period referred to a body of concepts constituting a metaphysical science.

With the Renaissance came the resurrection of the lost Greco-Roman books of magick. In particular, the Renaissance produced the great Hermetic teachings which are the foundations for many modern magickal teachings and traditions. The Hermetic books, originally written in Greek sometime around the third century, appeared in a pseudo-Egyptian style or form. These texts preserved the ancient teachings of Persia, Chaldea, India, and the Greek Mystery Cults. As a body of accumulated teachings they were heavily influenced by Neoplatonism, Gnosticism, and Neopythagoreanism. The occult manuscripts of the Renaissance period laid the foundation for the magickal texts that appeared throughout all of Europe.

In 1460 Cosimo de Medici came into possession of many Hermetic manuscripts from Macedonia and the waning Byzantine Empire. He ordered Marsilio Ficino (an Italian philosopher and theologian) to translate these texts, and through his efforts we now possess a body of occult knowledge that is still the basis for magickal thought. In the latter period of the Renaissance these magickal texts appear in France, England and Germany. In northern Europe, English player groups and Mummers spread the magickal views of Hermetic knowledge as they traveled about the countryside. Some people believe that the Shakespearean players were among the most active in this pursuit.

Neoplatonism, a philosophy based on the teachings of Plato, also influenced European magick. Plotinus, a Hellenized Egyptian, brought about this revival circa A.D. 244 Plotinian Neoplatonism was itself revived in fifteenth-century Italy by Marsilio Ficino. John Colet is credited with introducing Neoplatonism into England which paved the way for the

Cambridge Platonists of the seventeenth century. The doctrines of Plotinus became the official teachings of the Platonic Academy and greatly influenced even Christian theology.

Many schools of Neoplatonism, such as the Pergamene, engaged in magickal practices (theurgy). By the fifth century such tenets became firmly established and influenced many friars and monks engaged in translating ancient texts. One such example is Tommaso Campanella, a seventeenth-century Dominican friar who was charged with heresy and imprisoned by the Church for trying to reconcile science and reason with Christian revelation. The monks and friars who, during the Middle Ages, wrote down the Celtic legends we now possess were no doubt knowledgeable in Neoplatonism. It is likely that as Roman Catholicism was brought into such places as Ireland, so too WERE the Mediterranean teachings influencing Christian theology. In late antiquity and early medieval times philosophies of various religious traditions were attracted to, and influenced by, Neoplatonic thought.

The nineteenth-century Occult Revival gave birth to the Gardnerian Wicca movement and was itself stimulated by the classical teachings revived during the Renaissance. The works of Giovanni Pico della Mirandola profoundly influenced Western Occultism. In 1486 Pico published his work *Conclusiones nongentae in omni genere scientiarum* (900 Conclusions in every kind of science) containing everything from natural philosophy to metaphysics, to the teachings of the Kabbalah.

Oriental philosophy merged with Western Occultism, modifying many of the ancient Aegean/Mediterranean concepts fundamental to Western magickal systems. The later works of Eliphas Levi, Francis Barrett, Franz Bardon, Aleister Crowley, A. E. Waite, Dion Fortune and MacGregor Mathers laid the foundation for the inner teachings of Gardner's personal magickal system. This is not to suggest that Wicca is something that Gerald Gardner invented, but rather to confirm that much of what he added to traditional Pagan beliefs came from such sources. Clearly, however, Wiccan Magick is also an evolution of Folk Magick traditions seen throughout all of Europe.

Glossary

AKASHA: In occult terms the pure and uncontaminated spirit emanating into the lower Planes from the Divine Plane.

AKASHIC RECORDS: An aspect of the Odic mantle in which all of the thoughts and deeds that have occurred on the Earth are stored in the magnetic field of its etheric atmosphere.

AOUR: The synthesis and equilibrium of the power of Od and Ob. The spiritual light arising from the balance of Od and Ob.

ASTRAL: A very refined nonphysical substance existing within the Astral Plane that is shaped around thoughts and concepts to create images or forms.

ASTRAL LIGHT: The *informing* intelligence of astral material that is the foundation on which all forms arrange themselves. Levi sometimes referred to it as the "Imagination of Nature."

ASTRAL PLANE: A dimension of a higher vibratory rate than the physical dimension, in which images form prior to manifestation in the physical world.

ATAVISTIC RESURGENCE: A spontaneous shift in consciousness in which primal natures are evoked inan individual from the deep recesses of the Collective Consciousness.

AURA: An etheric energy field surrounding a body. It is a composite of mental and spiritual attributes of the indwelling spirit inhabiting the body.

CHAKRA: One of seven zones of occult energy within the human body.

CONE OF POWER: An energy field composed of the electromagnetic energies of the practitioners creating it. It is typically envisioned as a cone shape rising in the middle of the ritual circle.

EGREGORE(S): Beings whose bodies are composed of Astral Light formed by a Cult of worshippers and animated by emanations from the Divine Plane. Gods and Goddesses as visualized by Humankind and given the breath of life by the Source of All Things. In this way human minds can comprehend something of Divine nature and establish a two-way communication.

ELEMENTS: In Western Occultism the Four Elements of Creation: Earth, Air, Fire, and Water. They are etheric substances reflected in material counterparts.

EQUILIBRIUM: The balancing of forces in their opposing activities. A magickal regulation of forces in motion. A reconciling of opposites.

ETHER: An *intangible* material substance as opposed to a spiritual substance. It often refers to an unseen vaporous substance, as well as to the occult counterpart of an atmosphere.

ETHERIC: Composed of Ether. An intangible force or substance. Sometimes used to differentiate between Spirit and Matter.

FAMILIAR: A spirit or elemental with whom one has a psychic and/or magickal rapport. Also a power animal form that is of a kindred nature.

GLYPH: A design depicting a principle or concept.

HERMETIC: Ancient teachings based on the concepts and principles taught by Pythagoras, Plato, and Hermes Trismegistus. Texts originating from the Mystery cults of the Aegean/Mediterranean as well as from Persia and Chaldea.

KABBALAH: An ancient Hebrew system of magickal and mystical philosophy.

KUNDALINI: Magickal power residing at the base of the spine. It is evoked through sexual and sensual energy.

MACROCOSM: The greater representation of something lesser.

MAGUS: One who is a master of the occult arts.

MANA: Raw unconscious energy that automatically responds to external stimuli. It is the accumulation of power within an object or a setting.

MICROCOSM: A miniature representation of something greater.

NEOPLATONISM: A philosophy based upon Platonism with elements of mysticism and Judaic/Christian concepts. It posits a single source from which all existence emanates and through which the soul can be mystically united.

NOUS: Universal Intelligence. An immaterial eternal spiritual entity involved in physical creation.

NUMEN: The conscious energy within an object or a place. The Numen taps into the accumulation of Mana and is responsible for occult phenomena and for various types of mysterious manifestations.

OB: The passive, negative, and receptive serpent force.

OD: The active, positive and initiating serpent force.

OLD WAYS: The pre-Christian European Mystery Cult teachings based upon the principles and concepts within Nature.

PLATONISM: The Philosophy of Plato, mainly the view asserting ideal forms as an absolute and eternal reality of which the phenomena of the world are an imperfect and transitory reflection.

PLOTINIAN: A form of Neoplatonism involving a more complex mystical overview. Basic to its tenets is the concept of the One Ultimate Principle from which emanates all others. Redemption of the soul through various levels of existence is another primary focus of this belief system.

PRANA: The Life Principle; the breath of life.

SCRYING: Divination by means of gazing into a dark reflective surface.

SIGIL: A concept or principle designed by magickal formula to contain the essence of something.

SYMBOL: An image that represents something else.

THOUGHT-FORM: Literally a thought transformed into a manifestation of itself in one form or another.

Suggested Reading

WICCA

To Ride a Silver Broomstick by Silver RavenWolf (Llewellyn).

The Witches' Way by Janet and Stewart Farrar (Hale).

The Secrets of Ancient Witchcraft by Arnold and Patricia Crowther (University).

Witchcraft: A Tradition Renewed by Doreen Valiente and Evan Jones (Phoenix).

Witchcraft from the Inside by Ray Buckland (Llewellyn).

Wicca: The Old Religion in the New Age by Vivianne Crowley (Aquarian).

MAGICK

Modern Magick by Donald M. Kraig (Llewellyn).

Initiation into Hemetics by Franz Bardon (Ruggeberg).

Inner Traditions of Magic by William Gray (Weiser).

The Tree of Life by Israel Regardie (Weiser).

The Golden Bough by James Frazer (MacMillan).

Stolen Lightning by Daniel L. O'Keefe (Vintage).

To Stir a Magick Cauldron by Silver RavenWolf (Llewellyn).

A Grimoire of Shadows by Ed Fitch (Llewellyn).

The Candle Magick Workbook by Kala and Ketz Pajeon (Citadel).

Practical Candleburning Rituals by Raymond Buckland (Llewellyn).

MYSTERY TEACHINGS

Woman's Mysteries by M. Esther Harding (Harper).

Celebrating the Male Mysteries by R. J. Stewart (Arcania).

The Cauldron of Change by De-Anna Alba (Delphi).

The Underworld Initiation by R. J. Stewart (Aquarian).

The Mysteries of Britain by Lewis Spence (Newcastle).

Mysteries of the Dark Moon by Demetra George (Harper).

The Ancient Mysteries;:A Source Book by Marvin Meyer (Harper).

The Secret Teachings of All Ages by Manly P. Hall (Philosophical Research Society).

The Golden Bough by James Frazer (MacMillan).

Earth Rites by Janet and Colin Bord (Granada).

MAGICKAL HERBS

The Magical & Ritual Use of Herbs by Richard Alan Miller (Destiny).

The Magical & Ritual Use of Aphrodisiacs by Richard Alan Miller (Destiny).

Cunningham's Encyclopedia of Magical Herbs by Scott Cunningham (Llewellyn).

Magical Herbalism by Scott Cunningham (Llewellyn).

Bibliography

Agrippa, Cornelius. *Three Books of Occult Philosophy.* Edited and annotated by Donald Typson. St. Paul: Llewellyn Publications, 1993.

Ankerloo, Bengt, and Gustav Henningsen, Editors. *Early Modern European Witchcraft: Centres and Peripheries.* London: Clarendon Press, 1993.

Bardon, Franz. *Initiation into Hermetics.* Wuppertal: Dieter Ruggeberg, 1971.

Butler, W. E. *The Magician: His Training and Work.* N. Hollywood: Wilshire Book Company, 1969.

Case, Paul F. *The Tarot: A Key to the Wisdom of the Ages.* Richmond: Macoy Publishing Company, 1947.

Cunningham, Scott. *Living Wicca: A Further Guide for the Solitary Practitioner.* St. Paul: Llewellyn, 1993.

———. *Cunningham's Encyclopedia of Magical Herbs.* St. Paul: Llewellyn, 1985.

Davidson, H. R. Ellis. *Myths and Symbols in Pagan Europe: Early Scandinavian and Celtic Religions.* Syracuse: Syracuse University Press, 1988.

Denning, Melita, and Osborne Phillips. *The Magical Philosophy,* volumes three and four. St. Paul: Llewellyn, 1975.

Evans-Wentz, W. Y. *The Fairy Faith in Celtic Countries.* New York: Citadel Press, 1994.

Farrar, Janet and Stewart. *The Witches' Way: Principles, Rituals and Beliefs of Modern Witchcraft.* London: Robert Hale, 1984.

————. *Spells And How They Work.* Custer: Phoenix Publishing Inc., 1990.

Fortune, Dion. *Applied Magic.* New York: Samuel Weiser, 1973.

————. *The Training and Work of an Initiate.* Wellingborough: The Aquarian Press, 1972.

Frazer, James G. *The Golden Bough: A Study in Magic and Religion.* New York: Macmillan Company, 1972.

Gale, Mort. *Moon Power.* New York: Warner Books, 1980.

Grant, Kenneth. *The Magical Revival.* New York: Samuel Weiser, 1972.

————. *Cults of the Shadow.* New York: Samuel Weiser, 1976.

Gray, William G. *Inner Traditions of Magic.* New York: Samuel Weiser, 1970.

————. *Western Inner Workings.* York Beach: Samuel Weiser, 1983.

Grieve, Mrs. M. *A Modern Herbal,* volumes one and two. New York: Dover Publications, 1971.

Harvey, Graham, and Charlotte. Hardman. *Paganism Today: Wiccans, Druids, the Goddess and Ancient Earth Traditions for the Twenty-First Century.* London: Thorsons, 1996.

Jones, Prudence and Pennick, Nigel. *A History of Pagan Europe.* London: Routledge, 1995.

Kaplan, Stuart R. *The Encyclopedia of Tarot,* volume 2. New York: U.S. Games Inc., 1986.

Kraig, Donald M. *Modern Magick: Eleven Lessons in the High Magickal Arts.* St. Paul: Llewellyn, 1988.

Leland, Charles. *Etruscan Magick & Occult Remedies.* New York: University Books, 1963

Levi, Eliphas. *The Key of the Mysteries*. London: Rider, 1984.

———. *Transcendental Magic*. New York: Samuel Weiser, 1974.

———. *The Great Secret*. New York: Samuel Weiser, 1975.

Luck, George. *Arcana Mundi: Magic and the Occult in the Greek and Roman Worlds*. Baltimore: Johns Hopkins University Press, 1986.

Luhrmann, T. M. *Persuasions of the Witch's Craft: Ritual Magic in Contemporary England*. Cambridge: Harvard University Press, 1989.

Meyer, Marvin W. (Editor). *The Ancient Mysteries, A Sourcebook: Sacred Texts of the Mystery Religions of the Ancient Mediterranean World*. San Francisco: Harper San Francisco, 1987.

O'Keefe, Daniel L. *Stolen Lightning: The Social Theory of Magic*. New York: Vintage Books, 1983.

Regardie, Israel. *The Tree of Life: A Study in Magic*. New York: Samuel Weiser, 1980.

Roney-Dougal, Serena. *Where Science and Magic Meet*. Longmead: Element, 1993.

Seligmann, Kurt. *The History of Magic and the Occult*. New York: Harmony Books, 1975.

Spence, Lewis. *Magic Arts in Celtic Britain*. London: The Aquarian Press, 1970.

Valiente, Doreen. *Natural Magic*. New York: St. Martin's Press, 1975.

———. *Witchcraft for Tomorrow*. London: Robert Hale Limited, 1978.

———. *The Rebirth of Witchcraft*. London: Robert Hale, 1989.

Index

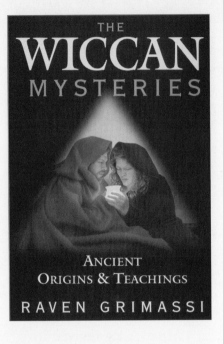

ITALIAN WITCHCRAFT
The Old Religion of Southern Europe

Raven Grimassi

(Formerly titled *Ways of the Strega*, revised and expanded)

Discover the rich legacy of magick and ritual handed down by Italian witches through the generations. Trace the roots of the Italian Pagan tradition as it survives the times, confronted by Christianity, revived in the 14th century by the Holy Strega, and passed on as the Legend of Aradia to the present day. Explore the secrets of Janarra (lunar) witches, Tanarra (star) witches, and Fanarra (ley lines) witches. Their ancient wisdoms come together in the modern Aridian tradition, presented here for both theoretical understanding and everyday practice. You will learn the gospel of Aradia, and the powerful practice of "casting shadows," an ancient tradition only now available to the public. *Italian Witchcraft* also gives you the practical how-tos of modern Strega traditions, including making tools, casting and breaking spells, seasonal and community rites, honoring the Watchers, creating a Spirit Flame, and much more.

1-56718-259-3
336 pp., 7¹/₂ x 9¹/₈, illus., softcover   **$14.95**

HEREDITARY WITCHCRAFT
Secrets of the Old Religion

Raven Grimassi

This book is about the Old Religion of Italy, and contains material that is at least 100 years old, much of which has never before been seen in print. This overview of the history and lore of the Hereditary Craft will show you how the Italian witches viewed nature, magick, and the occult forces. Nothing in this book is mixed with, or drawn from, any other Wiccan traditions.

The Italian witches would gather beneath the full moon to worship a goddess (Diana) and a god (Dianus). The roots of Italian Witchcraft extend back into the pre-history of Italy, in the indigenous Mediterranean/Aegean neolithic cult of the Great Goddess. Follow its development to the time of the Inquisition, when it had to go into hiding to survive, and to the present day. Uncover surprising discoveries of how expressions of Italian Witchcraft have been taught and used in this century.

1-56718-256-9, 7 ½ x 9 ⅛, 288 pp., 31 illus. $14.95

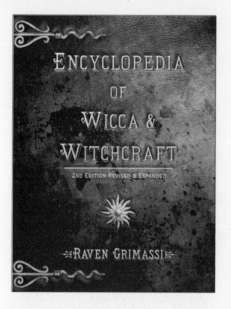

ENCYCLOPEDIA OF WICCA & WITCHCRAFT

Raven Grimassi

This indispensable reference work provides both a historical and cultural foundation for modern Wicca and Witchcraft, and it is the first to be written by an actual practitioner of the Craft.

Other encyclopedias present a series of surface topics such as tools, sabbats, Witchcraft trials, and various mundane elements. Unique to this encyclopedia is its presentation of Wicca/Witchcraft as a spiritual path, connecting religious concepts and spirituality to a historical background and a modern system of practice. It avoids the inclusion of peripheral entries typically included, and deals only with Wicca/Witchcraft topics, old and new, traditional and eclectic. It also features modern Wiccan expressions, sayings, and terminology. Finally, you will find a storehouse of information on European folklore and Western Occultism as related to modern Wicca/Witchcraft.

1-56718-257-7
28 pp., 8 x 10, 300+ illus. & photos   **$24.95**

SPIRIT OF THE WITCH
Religion & Spirituality in Contemporary Witchcraft

Raven Grimassi

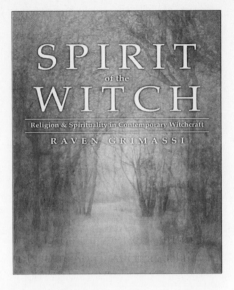

Find peace and happiness in the spiritual teachings of the Craft...
What is in the spirit of the Witch? What empowers Witches in their daily and spiritual lives? How does a person become a Witch?

In *Spirit of the Witch*, Raven Grimassi, an initiate of several Wiccan traditions, reveals the Witch as a citizen living and working like all others—and as a spiritual being who seeks alignment with the natural world. He provides an overview of the Witch's view of deity and how it manifests in the cycles of nature. Seasonal rituals, tools, magic, and beliefs are all addressed in view of their spiritual underpinnings. Additionally, he shows the relationship among elements of pre-Christian European religion and modern Witchcraft beliefs, customs, and practices.

- The first book devoted entirely to the theme of spirituality in Witchcraft
- Explores the spiritual elements of the rituals, practices, and beliefs of Witchcraft
- Includes the oral tradition of Witches, as well as cultural, literary, anthropological, and historical connections

0-7387-0338-9
288 pp., 6 x 9, glossary, bibliog.,index $12.95